THINGS TO COME

Biblical Prophecy in Common Language

Dr. Danny L. Moody

WESTBOW
PRESS®
A DIVISION OF THOMAS NELSON
& ZONDERVAN

WestBow Press books may be ordered through booksellers or by contacting:

WestBow Press
A Division of Thomas Nelson & Zondervan
1663 Liberty Drive
Bloomington, IN 47403
www.westbowpress.com
1 (866) 928-1240

Because of the dynamic nature of the Internet, any web addresses or links contained in this book may have changed since publication and may no longer be valid. The views expressed in this work are solely those of the author and do not necessarily reflect the views of the publisher, and the publisher hereby disclaims any responsibility for them.

Any people depicted in stock imagery provided by Thinkstock are models, and such images are being used for illustrative purposes only. Certain stock imagery © Thinkstock.

ISBN: 978-1-5127-0517-1 (sc)
ISBN: 978-1-5127-0518-8 (hc)
ISBN: 978-1-5127-0516-4 (e)

Library of Congress Control Number: 2015911931

Print information available on the last page.

WestBow Press rev. date: 8/18/2015

Contents

Acknowledgments

I am indebted to so very many people who have encouraged me not only to write *Things To Come* but who also have provided invaluable help to me in making it become a reality. I am certain that I will be guilty of leaving someone out who should be mentioned, but please know that it was not done intentionally.

First and foremost, I want to thank my Lord and Savior Jesus Christ for the wonderful and eternal salvation that He has secured and given freely to me. I am humbled and honored that He would then call me to the ministry and allow me to serve Him in a full-time capacity for more than thirty years. It is to Him alone that I would defer any and all the glory that might possibly be gained from this endeavor.

I want to thank my wonderful wife Sherry for being patient with me concerning the time away that I needed to get the book finished. Her partnership in ministry and life has been invaluable to me for almost four decades. Sherry, You Are the Best!

My dear friends Gary and Pat McGee have been very generous in allowing me to use their guesthouse as a refuge and wonderful place to get alone with God, my books, and my computer to write. I cannot adequately express how much I appreciate their gracious spirit and faithful friendship. You Guys Are Life-Long Friends!

Finally, I want to express a special word of thanks to my Executive Assistant, Brenda Miller, for the many hours that she has put in on this project. This book would not have been possible without her help with editing, formatting, communicating with publishers, and any other thing needed to make it through the production process. Thank You, Brenda!

Foreword

Dr. D.L. Moody has done us a great service. In a day when many are calling into question the basic Bible truths relative to the return of Christ, he has given us this excellent volume.

The book is biblically faithful. You will find many, many biblical references that support the pre-millennial, pre-tribulation view presented here. Dr. Moody clearly points out that this view has the most biblical support. The reader will receive a good Bible survey of the pertinent passages relative to the subjects discussed in this helpful volume.

Also, there is a great need for a book to lay out in a simple, easy-to-understand format the Bible doctrines of the rapture, the tribulation, etc. Dr. Moody's volume certainly does this for us.

I was also blessed by the many helpful illustrations Dr. Moody gives to illuminate the truths set forth here. The preacher and Bible teachers in general will find a wealth of help in teaching the doctrines of the return of Christ.

I am pleased to recommend this volume to you. I pray it will have a broad readership and will result in believers being built up in the faith and many unsaved people coming to know Christ as their Savior.

Jerry Vines
Pastor-Emeritus, First Baptist Church, Jacksonville, Florida
Two-time President, the Southern Baptist Convention
President, Jerry Vines Ministries, Inc.

Where is God? ... I am glad you asked!

Where is God? Where is God in the midst of a world filled with war, violence, wickedness, religious turmoil, financial tension, and a million more despairing issues? Has He lost control of what He has created? Has He diminished in power and sovereignty that He once possessed? If neither of these is true, how long will He allow such calamity to continue?

To an unbelieving world, these questions may seem to have merit when offered the concept of an All-Powerful, All-Knowing, All-Caring God. To view current global situations without a firm faith in the Word of God and the God of the Word, doubt and anxiety are certainly understandable. However, to those who have found the joy and assurance that come from a living and lively relationship with God through a personal relationship with Jesus Christ, what we see in the nightly news creates an air of excitement. This excitement is because God Himself has given us a prophetic glimpse of the signs and times that will happen as we approach the last days of human history as we have known it.

Since the fall of man in Genesis 3, sin has been causing pain, sorrow, confusion, and chaos among God's prized creation, mankind. As population increased and nations developed, these undesirable consequences of sin have grown and manifested themselves in a constant elevation of size and scope, leading to a horrific spiral in the 21st century.

Where is God in all of this? **He is still on His throne and in complete control of all that goes on here on planet earth!** Has His glory and power somehow faded over the course of these past 6,000 years? **Never in a million years (and more)!** He is "the same yesterday, and today, and forever" (Heb. 13:8). How long will He allow all of this to continue? ... **Well, I am glad you asked!**

For Bible believers, three bedrock beliefs have sustained us and continue to be our source of confidence ... "the Book, the Blood, and the Blessed Hope." The Word of God is our eternal source of information, instruction, and inspiration. From it, we learn where we came from, what we can expect, what is expected of us, and where we are going from here. The blood of Jesus Christ is the covering for all our sin and what brings us into a personal and eternal relationship with the God of the universe. Through faith in Jesus Christ and His completed work of salvation on the cross, we become a part of the family of God. As children of God, we know our Heavenly Father cares about and cares for His kids. His care reaches us now in troubled times and allows us to share in triumphant times that are yet to come.

Finally, we rest in the Blessed Hope ... the Second Coming of Jesus Christ. Through the ages, believers have suffered persecution from the wicked, scoffing from the "wise of this world," and overall disregard from those who "believed not the truth, but had pleasure in unrighteousness" (2 Thess. 2:12). Yet, we continue to contend that according to the scriptures, Jesus Christ will return one day and there will be a global and eternal reckoning for nations and individuals alike.

Rejection of the biblical teachings of the Second Coming reaches back to the writing of the New Testament. Led by the Holy Spirit, the Apostle Peter addresses the issue, and his message is preserved and relevant for the times in which we live:

> This second epistle, beloved, I now write unto you; in both which I stir up your pure minds by way of remembrance: That ye may be mindful of the words which were spoken before by the holy prophets, and of the commandment of us the apostles of the Lord and Saviour: Knowing this first, that there shall come in the last days scoffers, walking after their own lusts, And saying, Where is the promise of his coming? for since the fathers fell asleep, all things continue as they were from the beginning of the creation. For this they willingly are ignorant of, that by the word of God the heavens were of old, and the earth standing out of the water and in the water: Whereby the world that then was, being overflowed with water, perished: But the heavens and the earth, which are now, by the same word are kept in store, reserved unto fire against the day of judgment and perdition of ungodly men. But, beloved, be not ignorant of this one thing, that one day is with the Lord as a thousand years, and a thousand years as one day. The Lord is not slack concerning his promise, as some men count slackness; but is longsuffering to us-ward, not

willing that any should perish, but that all should come to repentance. (2 Pet. 3:1-9)

Concerning the Second Coming and the judgment of the world, Peter points out:

1. The prophets and apostles announce it (vs. 2)
2. The scoffers renounce it (vs. 3-4)
3. History proves it can happen (i.e. ... The Flood vs. 5-6)
4. Time does not diminish the reality of it (vs. 7-8)
5. Delay is only because of the longsuffering nature of God (vs. 9)

The most common response of those who are unwilling to accept any suggestion that Christ will return to judge the wicked as well as reward the righteous is they have heard that for years and it has not happened yet. While the words of their statement are true, their defiance toward the message is a terrible, grave, and eternal mistake. Innumerable examples can be given of events which were doubted to ever possibly happen and yet they did.

The chapters you are about to read are not for convincing you of the Second Coming of Christ. Instead, they are designed to give you, the reader, an overview of what the Bible teaches concerning last days, including events, personalities, geographical locations (both on earth and in heaven), as well as motivating forces both physical and spiritual that will be prevalent during the final days of mankind's existence on earth.

The theological term that is used for what we will be discussing is *eschatology*, which means "the study of last things or days." You will notice, however, that there are few theological terms used in this writing, and that is by design. The basic truths of eschatology can and should be understood by the average church member who wishes to have a working knowledge of things yet to happen.

A primary subject of the Bible is the Second Coming of Christ. Some scholars have calculated that there are at least 315 references to the Second Coming in the New Testament alone. With such emphasis placed upon the subject, every believer would do well to be informed about it, expecting it, and looking forward to seeing and being with our Savior.

The scope of our study will begin at the rapture, carry us through the Tribulation Period and the Battle of Armageddon, and ultimately to the eternal state of both the believer and the unbeliever. Unlike a complete commentary on this subject, there may be details of events that are not covered. However, by the time you finish reading, you should have a good idea of what the Bible tells us about what is yet ahead concerning the Blessed Hope.

By the way, are you still asking, "Where is God?" Well, I am glad you asked! You are about to see just where He is and what He is about to do. Soon the whole world will know that God is alive and well. Soon Paul's words to the Philippians concerning Jesus Christ will be fully accomplished:

> Wherefore God also hath highly exalted him, and
> given him a name which is above every name: That
> at the name of Jesus every knee should bow, of

things in heaven, and things in earth, and things under the earth; And that every tongue should confess that Jesus Christ is Lord, to the glory of God the Father. (Phil. 2:9-11)

CHAPTER 1

The Rapture

In 1996, a nine-year-old girl by the name of Amber Hagerman was abducted while riding her bicycle in Arlington, Texas, the city where the college I work for is located. I remember the tension and anxiety that enveloped the city during the search for Amber. The FBI was called in to aid in the search, and the news media was constantly reporting on the case. Sadly, after four days, her little body was found in a drainage ditch. To add to the tragedy, her killer was never found. Our tension and anxiety quickly turned to mourning for the family of this precious little one.

Out of this tragic situation, however, came the development of a child-abduction alert system where the dissemination of information about missing children is quickly carried through several media outlets. This system is now known as the AMBER Alert, or America's Missing: Broadcast Emergency Response, in memory of our own Amber Hagerman. This system has been used many times since its origination and has been responsible for helping to find and bring many children safely home to their fear-filled families. Amber can never be replaced, but out of her tragedy has come something positive.

I tell you this story because of one word that is associated with it: *missing,* a close cousin to the word *unknown.* In the case of a missing person, we know they are somewhere, but we do not know where. Fear sets in, and imagination starts forming terrible possibilities. All we know for certain is that the person is missing.

One person missing is perplexing enough. But can you imagine what it would be like if, all of a sudden, hundreds of thousands or even millions of individuals disappeared without a trace? Men, women, boys, and girls ... *missing!* Television stations would likely have the story as its lead or perhaps only story. Alerts would be sent by radio, Internet, and lighted highway signs reading, "Missing!" Businesses, manufacturing plants, hospitals, emergency-response teams, airlines, schools, and every other form of societal mechanics would be affected. These people would have to be somewhere, but where?

Could this ever happen? Yes! It not only *could* happen, but it *will* happen!

The next great event on God's time calendar is what we call the rapture of the saints. This event will mark the beginning of the end of this world's systems. If we knew the time this is to occur, marking a date for the end of the world would become feasible. However, Jesus has told us in Matthew 24:36, "But of that day and hour knoweth no man, no, not the angels of heaven, but my Father only."

We use the word *rapture* because it simply means "catching away or snatching out." This is precisely what will happen to all born-again believers who are alive at the time Jesus comes for His children. We call this event imminent (due to happen at any time), for there are no prophecies in scripture yet to be fulfilled before this can occur. Right now, the stage is perfectly set for Jesus Christ to return in the rapture and call us unto Himself.

The second coming of Christ will occur in two phases. We might call the first phase the rapture and the second phase the return. In the first phase, Jesus will return for the bodies of departed saints of God (whom He will raise and change) and for living saints who are alive at the time of His coming (whom He will also change). The second phase will be at the end of the tribulation period (seven years later) when He returns to judge the wicked (covered in chapter 4) and the saints will be with Him. For clarification, you might think of it this way:

- At the rapture, Christ will return in the air *for* His saints.
- At the return, Christ will return to the earth *with* His saints.

When the rapture occurs, it will set in motion all of the prophecies concerning the time known as the tribulation period; these seven years are covered in Revelation 6–19, as well as many mentions by Old Testament prophets, New Testament writers, and by Jesus Himself.

There are three differing views when it comes to the rapture as it pertains to the whole of the tribulation:

1. Mid-Tribulation Rapture—This view teaches that the tribulation, which is seven years in length, will begin, and at the mid-way point of the tribulation (three and one-half years later), Christ will return to rapture the saints.
2. Post-Tribulation Rapture—This view teaches that the believers will go through the whole tribulation and then Christ will return to rapture them out.

3. Pre-Tribulation Rapture—This view teaches that the believers will be taken out prior to the beginning of the tribulation period and that this event will actually mark the beginning of it.

The Pre-Tribulation rapture seems to have the most biblical support. A few reasons for taking this view follow:

1. Scriptural mention of deliverance from God's "wrath to come"

> And to wait for his Son from heaven, whom he raised from the dead, even Jesus, which delivered us from the wrath to come. (1 Thess. 1:10)

> For God hath not appointed us to wrath, but to obtain salvation by our Lord Jesus Christ, Who died for us, that, whether we wake or sleep, we should live together with him. (1 Thess. 5:9–10)

> The context in both of these passages has to do with the second coming, and the phrase "wrath to come" is almost always associated with the tribulation.

2. No mention of the church during the tribulation period

> Even though there are numerous mentions of the church in the first four chapters of Revelation, from chapters 6 to 19—the passages that deal with the tribulation period—the church is not mentioned. The subject of the church is prominent in most all of

the New Testament and is always closely tied to Jesus Christ. The church remains prominent in the first three chapters of Revelation, with Jesus writing letters to the seven churches of Asia. However, in Revelation 4:1, John is called to heaven (an indication of the rapture occurring), and there is no mention again of the church. What is called the church age ends at Revelation 4:1, as believers are now with Christ, caught up in the rapture.

3. Kings call their "ambassadors" home before a war

Though lacking an actual biblical reference, the logic of this makes perfect sense and would be consistent with our relationship with God, as Christians are described as "Ambassadors for Christ" on earth (2 Cor. 5:20). We are also told that God will one day declare war on the wickedness of the world. Before a king declares war, he first calls his ambassadors home for their protection and safety. So it would make sense that God will call us unto Himself before the conflict of the tribulation begins.

Christians all over the globe will be noticeably missing. For those left on earth following the rapture, an incredible mystery will occur. Husbands will have wives and wives will have husbands who will suddenly be missing. Parents will have children and children will have parents who will suddenly be missing. Coworkers, neighbors, classmates, and friends will rush to file a missing persons report. Thousands of church buildings will be abandoned, but perhaps a few will continue with business as usual. There will be cars without a driver, airplanes without a pilot, courtrooms without a judge, classrooms without a teacher, patrol cars without a police officer, department stores without a clerk, and a million more immediate and noticeable vacancies that were once occupied by followers of Jesus Christ. All of them ... *missing!*

In fact, the present-day popularity of movies about invasions of space aliens and body snatchers and the increased interest in UFOs and life on other planets might very well be the accounts people consider to explain what has happened. I am not sure, however, that these will validate why only the "Jesus people" were taken. We do know that God will send the remaining rejecting populace a "strong delusion" (2 Thess. 2:11), but what this delusion will be is unknown.

Questions from those left behind will abound. "Who took them? Where did they take them? What are they doing to them?" Here are the answers: Jesus took them ... to a meeting in the air and then to heaven ... where they will be with Him and enjoy Him forever! They will be missing from the earth but joyfully present with the Lord.

Leading up to the Rapture

As previously mentioned, the time in which we now live is called the church age. The majority of the books of the New Testament are written in relation to the church and, because of inspiration from the Holy Spirit, the writings are relevant to churches in the 21st century. I hold to the view that the church age began in Matthew 16:18 with Jesus' statement to Peter: "Upon this rock I will build my church; and the gates of hell shall not prevail against it." The church was then commissioned in Matthew 28:19 with what is commonly called the Great Commission, empowered by the Holy Spirit on the day of Pentecost in Acts 2, and continues until the event recorded in Revelation 4:1, the rapture.

The question often asked is "Are we living in the last days?" To answer that question, I believe we must turn to the Word of God. Within the pages of God-inspired scripture, we are given signs and indications that point to the triumphant return of Jesus Christ. After exploring these biblical signs and assessing our current global conditions, I conclude that the stage is perfectly set for the rapture to occur and all end-time prophecies to begin to unfold. Let us look at a few indicators that bring us to the rapture:

1. Scoffers will come

> Knowing this first, that there shall come in the last days scoffers, walking after their own lusts, And saying, Where is the promise of his coming? for since the fathers fell asleep, all things continue as they were from the beginning of the creation. (2 Pet. 3:3-4)

> As previously addressed, there are those who would rather not accept the message of the coming judgment of God. Their "own lust" causes them to prefer a business-as-usual mentality where no accountability to a Holy God exists.

The word that Peter uses here, translated *scoffers*, carries with it the idea of mocking. In the last days, many will make fun of anything that has to do with the Second Coming. Sadly, those who hold to a literal and bold stand for the coming of Christ are often labeled as non-intellectuals and fanatics, not taken seriously, and seen as out-of-touch with reality. Adding to the tragedy of this defamation, the pulpits are all too often silent when it comes to teaching and preaching on the Second Coming, choosing to spend their efforts on felt needs instead of eternal needs. Preaching boldly that Jesus Christ is coming and individuals must be ready to meet Him is indeed unpopular. However, if the Bible is our message and its teachings emphatically declare an imminent rapture and following judgment, then faithfully and boldly instructing our congregations about it is the only recourse.

In recent years, date-setters among some who claim to be Christian scholars have not helped. As previously stated, no man knows the hour or the day of His return. Every time a date is set and proves to be wrong, the mocking increases. The fact that they were proven wrong does not, however, invalidate the biblical fact of Jesus' soon return.

2. Selfishness and Materialism will abound

> This know also, that in the last days perilous times shall come. For men shall be lovers of their own selves, covetous, boasters, proud, blasphemers,

disobedient to parents, unthankful, unholy, Without natural affection, trucebreakers, false accusers, incontinent, fierce, despisers of those that are good, Traitors, heady, highminded, lovers of pleasures more than lovers of God; Having a form of godliness, but denying the power thereof: from such turn away. (2 Tim. 3:1-5)

And unto the angel of the church of the Laodiceans write; These things saith the Amen, the faithful and true witness, the beginning of the creation of God; I know thy works, that thou art neither cold nor hot: I would thou wert cold or hot. So then because thou art lukewarm, and neither cold nor hot, I will spue thee out of my mouth. Because thou sayest, I am rich, and increased with goods, and have need of nothing; and knowest not that thou art wretched, and miserable, and poor, and blind, and naked (Rev. 3:14-17)

Many scholars believe that the Laodicean church also pictures the condition of Christianity in general in the last days of the Church Age. This could well be and if so, then one mark of the end times will be the mentality that material goods are all we need.

One needs little convincing that our society at large holds to a very self-centered, selfish, and materialistic mindset. America is quickly becoming a welfare state with an out-of-control federal financial debt that— even if all excessive spending ended today—would take decades to repay. This philosophy has as its core the idea of "Take care of ME" or "ME first, regardless of ramifications."

Credit card indebtedness of individuals and families has skyrocketed over the past few decades. As one financial expert has been famously quoted as saying, "We spend money we do not have, on things we do not need, to impress people we do not like."

Morality is being redefined on a global scale. Lifestyles that once would never have been acceptable are now common. Trust and honesty are now measured on a sliding scale of what is most convenient and self-serving at the time. The family unit is often filled with dissatisfaction, division, and divorce. The idea of parental authority over children and children being obedient to their parents has become an archaic standard. Basically, any kind of authority is disdained and freedom of personal choice without restraint is celebrated.

Lest I be guilty of merely cursing the darkness, let me light a candle. Jesus Christ, God's only Son, has come to set us free from the bondage and chaos that sin makes. The situation that has just been described is a result of sin and the consequences of people who forget God. Having a personal relationship with Jesus is the only enabling power for a person to live in the midst of an out-of-control world and not allow the world to control him. For the child of God, "hope springs eternal" primarily because our Blessed Hope, the rapture, is just ahead.

3. Unwillingness to hear the truth

> For the time will come when they will not endure sound doctrine; but after their own lusts shall they heap to themselves teachers, having itching ears; And they shall turn away their ears from the truth, and shall be turned unto fables. (2 Tim. 4:3-4)

Having served as a senior pastor for over 20 years, I can almost feel the cringe of young Timothy as Paul gave him this word of forewarning. A man with a pastor's heart desires to love people and have people love him in return. One of the greatest heartbreaks a pastor ever experiences is to have a person or group of people leave his church, especially if their reason for leaving is a doctrinal issue. A pastor is accountable to God for faithfully proclaiming biblical truth in a spirit of love and compassion for those he is instructing.

Paul's message was certainly relevant in the first century as Timothy served in the church at Ephesus. No doubt, Timothy experienced those of his own congregation who abandoned the truth he preached for falsehoods being taught in this city where paganism abounded. Twenty centuries later, turning from the truth to religious experiences that appeal to the flesh is as disconcerting and tragic as it was in Timothy's days as a pastor.

In today's world, feeling sincere has replaced submitting to absolute truth in religious circles. This has given rise to numerous strange beliefs and practices, all in the name of religion. Biblical truth is no longer essential among many and is even mocked, ridiculed, and declared obsolete among the adherents of religious groups. To these, what makes a person feel good about himself and brings no discomfort to his way of life is more important than what God has declared.

"Churches" have even been started to satisfy individual yearnings to be spiritual but not deny one's individual preferences, regardless of what those preferences may be. Examples of this include the New Age Movement, Homosexual Churches, Scientology, Church-in-a-Pub, and just about any other diversion or desire you can think of. It seems that outrageous is in and orthodoxy is out.

I am not insinuating that church can only be done in a building with four walls and a steeple, or with first, second, and last verses of a hymn. The truth, however, remains the same in every generation and culture. Isaiah's assessment of a backslidden Israel sounds so much like America's relationship with truth today:

> For our transgressions are multiplied before thee, and our sins testify against us: for our transgressions are with us; and as for our iniquities, we know them; In transgressing and lying against the LORD, and departing away from our God, speaking oppression and revolt, conceiving and uttering from the heart words of falsehood. And judgment is turned away backward, and justice standeth afar off: for truth

is fallen in the street, and equity cannot enter. Yea, truth faileth; and he that departeth from evil maketh himself a prey: and the LORD saw it, and it displeased him that there was no judgment. (Isa. 59:12-15)

The closer we get to the coming of the Savior at the rapture, the more churches and individual church members should be committed to biblical truth and should be unapologetically contending for it.

4. Increase in knowledge and mobility

But thou, O Daniel, shut up the words, and seal the book, even to the time of the end: many shall run to and fro, and knowledge shall be increased. (Dan. 12:4)

One of the timeless treasures of the Word of God is its Old Testament prophecies about the last days, made hundreds of years before the first coming of Jesus Christ. More than 500 years before Christ's birth, Daniel gives us a glimpse of what to expect in "the time of the end." Does this not speak to the divinely inspired nature of the Bible?

In this passage, Daniel points out two characteristics of the last days. First, he states that "many shall run to and fro," speaking about the mobility of the earth's populous. Over the course of 6,000 years of human history, travel remained pretty much the same for every culture and generation—by walking, horseback or donkey, wagons, boats, and the like. Only in the last 100 years has transportation dramatically changed. With the advent of the train, automobile, and airplane, traveling great distances has now become an everyday affair. No one in Daniel's day, the early Church Age, or even the 19th century would have ever dreamed of travel as we know it today.

In his notes on "Last Days," the late Dr. Jerry Falwell gives the following, now humorous, account concerning Daniel 12:4:

> After reading this passage many years ago, the great scientist-Christian Sir Isaac Newton is reported to have said: *'Personally I cannot help but believe that these words refer to the end times. Men will travel from country to country in an unprecedented manner. There may be some inventions which will enable people to travel much more quickly than they do now'.*
>
> This was written around 1680 A.D. Newton went on to speculate that this speed might actually exceed 50 m.p.h. Some eighty years later, the famous French atheist, Voltaire, read Newton's words and retorted: *'See what a fool Christianity makes of an otherwise brilliant man! Here a scientist like Newton actually writes that men may travel at the rate of 30 or 40 m.p.h. Has he forgotten that if man would travel at this rate he would be suffocated? His heart would stand still!'* (Falwell)

Further, travel is no longer limited to crossing land and sea, but we now live in the age of space travel. "Running to and fro" has taken on a whole new meaning.

Secondly, Daniel points out that "knowledge shall be increased." Granted, over the course of human history, knowledge gradually increased and technological advances were made in every generation. However, who could have ever dreamed that the rate of increase in these areas would get to the point we are experiencing today? Every segment of our society is affected by the whirlwind of advances: medicine and medical research, electronics and engineering, communications and media, and the lists get longer by the minute. A computer bought six months ago is out of date; a cell phone that is more than a year old is not "cool" anymore; and sitting on your couch to watch television is old school because you can now carry a TV wherever you go.

The Prophet Daniel may have lived more than 2,500 years ago, but he certainly nailed that one!

5. The words of Jesus concerning last days

Jesus spoke much and often about the end of times, which created questions in the minds of His disciples, who were ever present and heard His teachings day after day.

Near the very end of Jesus' earthly ministry, perhaps a few days or weeks before His arrest, Peter,

James, John, and Andrew came to Jesus privately and inquired about these things that they had been hearing from Him. Their questions were of personal interest to the disciples since they had left all and had been following Him for the past three years. If the end was near, then they wanted to have all the information they could get about it. Jesus had even mentioned that the temple was going to be destroyed, a point of major significance to all the Jews—especially to the twelve who were followers of the One who prophesied that it would occur.

Jesus is sitting on the Mount of Olives when these disciples come to Him with two very important questions: "when shall these things be? And what shall be the sign of thy coming, and of the end of the world?" (Mat. 24:3). Matthew records in chapters 24 and 25 what has become known as the Olivet Discourse because of the location where it was delivered (also recorded in Mark's and Luke's gospels). These two chapters, some of the most descriptive passages in the Bible concerning world conditions and events in the last days, are spoken by none other than Jesus Himself.

Entire commentaries can be written on what Jesus describes about the coming of the end. By looking at only a few of the conditions, we can make the connection to indicators that we are living in the last days:

- " ...wars and rumours of wars" (Mat 24:6)
- " ...nation shall rise against nation, and kingdom against kingdom" (Mat 24:7)

- " ...famines and pestilences" (Mat 24:7)
- " ...earthquakes in divers places" (Mat 24:7)
- " ...false prophets shall rise, and shall deceive many" (Mat 24:11)
- " ...the love of many shall wax cold" (Mat 24:12)

When harmonizing the Olivet Discourse with John's account in The Revelation, it is apparent that most of what Jesus says here will happen during the Tribulation Period.

In Matthew's account of the Olivet Discourse, he records Jesus' answer to the question, "what shall be the sign of thy coming, and of the end of the world," but he does not answer the second, "when shall these things be?" Matthew simply records Jesus' warning that we should all be "ready" when it happens.

Luke, however, answers the second question:

And when these things begin to come to pass, then look up, and lift up your heads; for your redemption draweth nigh. (Luke 21:28)

These vital words relate to the believer and the rapture. Notice that Jesus warns that "when these things *begin* to come to pass" then "your redemption draweth nigh" (emphasis added). The word translated *redemption* is the Greek word *apolutrosis,* which implies "releasing, deliverance, and liberation."

The question then is, "Have these things begun to happen?" The obvious answer is "Yes ... Absolutely yes!" Some will argue, "These things have happened for the past two thousand years," and they are absolutely right. However, never in the past two thousand years have these things been happening with the intensity and frequency they are today. Consider the following:

- Wars going on in the world have become so commonplace that we rarely even think about them.
- National Security is a top priority in virtually every nation in the world; no nation really knows who is friendly or not. When you add the threat of nuclear weapons, no nation is truly safe.
- Action Against Hunger International reports on their website that *"Global hunger now afflicts nearly one billion people worldwide. Severe acute malnutrition, however, is the more immediate killer: it threatens the lives of 19 million children. Every year 3.5 million of them die from malnutrition-related causes"* (Action Against Hunger International).
- The United States Geological Survey reports that *"Earthquakes pose significant risk to 75 million Americans in 39 states."* They also report: *"The USGS estimates that several million earthquakes occur in the world each year, but many go undetected because they occur in remote areas or have very small magnitudes. The USGS*

now locates about 50 each day; 20,000 a year" (U.S. Geological Survey). These numbers have increased over the last 20 years, only partially due to the increase in seismograph stations in the world.

- New Religious Movements, or NRM's, are on the increase. These groups usually have their own doctrines, governments, rituals, and meeting places. Many of these use the internet for attracting and discipling their converts. Most of them have their own form of messiah or "Christ."

- While vibrant, evangelistic Christianity may be exercised in some local geographical areas or individual churches, it is declining on the global scale ... "the love of many shall wax cold." (Mat. 24:12)

Given the current world conditions, the dismal prospects that the Christians may find themselves in should indeed cause a greater anticipation of the appearance of Jesus Christ to take them home.

6. Israel is now a nation and back in her land

This may very well be the greatest indicator of all that our generation may be the people who are "alive and remain" at the time Jesus returns in the rapture. By doing an even casual reading of the book of The Revelation, if it is possible to read it casually, one can see that the nation of Israel is front-and-center for all that happens during the Tribulation Period. For the prophecies relating to this period to happen as recorded, Israel must "be a nation" and "be in the land" … both are true *right now*.

After almost 2,000 years of the Jewish people being scattered around the globe, the statehood of Israel was declared on May 14, 1948. Immediately the re-birthed nation had to fight the Arab nations to maintain its status as a nation and, since then, have had to do so time and again. In these battles, which were often against seemingly impossible odds, God miraculously intervened. Through unexplainable circumstances He protected, preserved, and brought victory to His people, Israel. Today, Israel stands as an independent and recognized nation among global powers. Jewish people are continually leaving countries around the world and returning to their homeland, making Israel stronger and more substantial with each transition.

It is no wonder that Israel is so prominent in the news today. This one small nation in the Middle East is constantly in the center of global controversy, but why? Israel is not the most populated nation in the world. It does not have the most powerful military force among the nations. Its land does not contain oil, precious metals, or gems. So why all the attention? It is for this reason: *what is happening in Israel is a biblical and spiritual matter.*

Israelites remain today as God's chosen people. God is now re-gathering and restoring them that He may fulfill His promises to them and prophecies concerning them. These two things will not be possible without conflict—enter the Tribulation Period events. Israel becoming a nation and her people returning to the land is likely the last piece of the puzzle for the beginning of the end.

So here we are! The stage is all set. All prophecies that needed to be fulfilled prior to the rapture have now been fulfilled. The clock is ticking and time is short! We must work while there is time to reach the lost around us; we must conduct ourselves in a fashion that we will not be ashamed at His appearing; we must keep our focus on eternally significant things; we must set our affections on things above and love His appearing.

One day, and maybe soon, we will hear the trumpet of God sound, the voice of the Archangel ring out, and on earth we will be declared to be *missing*!

Leaving at the Rapture

With the stage set on earth and nothing lacking prophetically to delay the rapture, the event will happen quickly. While the signs and indicators of that day may give us great reason to anticipate the rapture, we must keep in mind that no man knows exactly when it will occur (Mat. 24:36). Plenty of biblical imperatives also teach us always to be ready (Mat. 24:44; 2 Pet. 3:11-12; 1 John 3:2-3).

Looking at verses in The Revelation reveals the dividing nature of the rapture as it relates to present and future. In chapter 1, John, from the Isle of Patmos, is caught up in the Spirit and introduced to his mission of being a heavenly reporter in this revelation of Jesus Christ:

> Write the things which thou hast seen, and the things which are, and the things which shall be hereafter (Rev. 1:19)

The "things which thou hast seen" references the vision that he has just had of Jesus Christ. Then he writes about "the things which are," or time in the present. Finally, he writes about "the things which shall be hereafter," or future events.

Beginning in chapter 2 of The Revelation, Jesus gives John a message to each of the seven churches in Asia. These seven letters cover all of chapters 2 and 3. These were seven literal churches, making them a part of the present or Church Age dispensation and perhaps even representative of various phases the Church Age goes through.

The division of times is presented in the opening verse of chapter 4. The Church Age closes at the end of chapter 3 and then John has this experience:

> After this I looked, and, behold, a door *was* opened in heaven: and the first voice which I heard *was* as it were of a trumpet talking with me; which said, Come up hither, and I will shew thee things which must be hereafter. (Rev. 4:1)

John hears the voice that says, "Come up hither" and is then told that he is about to see "things which must be hereafter." John's experience here so closely resembles the rapture event that it cannot be coincident. Remember that in Revelation 1:19 John is told he would be writing about things that "are" or "present" – the Church Age; he is called now to heaven (at least a representation of the rapture); and he is about to see things that are "hereafter" or "future." The rapture is what separates the Church Age from the Tribulation; chapters 2-3 are present and chapters 4-22 are future.

Two primary passages describe how the rapture will take place: 1 Corinthians 15:51-58 and 1 Thessalonians 4:13-18. These two passages establish a chronological order of how it happens:

1. Jesus will return in the clouds

    At the precise time appointed by God and known only by God, Jesus Christ will step out of Heaven and come back to our domain, not to the earth but in the air above the earth. This act fulfils the prophecy given by the angel when Jesus ascended to heaven after His resurrection:

    And when he had spoken these things, while they beheld, he was taken up; and a cloud received him out of their sight. And while they looked stedfastly toward heaven as he went up, behold, two men stood by them in white apparel; Which also said, Ye men of Galilee, why stand ye gazing up into heaven? this same Jesus, which is taken up from you into heaven, shall so come in like manner as ye have seen him go into heaven. (Acts 1:9-11)

Though He will be unseen by the unbelieving world, His return will be a literal, physical, and bodily return in His glorified body.

2. The trumpet of God will sound

The trumpet seems to be God's instrument of choice. Throughout scripture, the trumpet is used for important and strategic events, including the rapture. Its primary use was to call an assembly:

And the LORD spake unto Moses, saying, Make thee two trumpets of silver; of a whole piece shalt thou make them: that thou mayest use them for the calling of the assembly, and for the journeying of the camps. And when they shall blow with them, all the assembly shall assemble themselves to thee at the door of the tabernacle of the congregation. (Num. 10:1-3)

In the Old Testament, two particular events involve the trumpet's use among God's people: to call to do battle and to call to worship. Both of these usages may come in to play with the sounding of the rapture trumpet because the greatest conflict ever known to man is about to happen on earth and the greatest worship experience ever held is about to take place in Heaven.

3. The archangel of God will shout

This archangel is probably Michael (Jude 9; Rev. 12:7). An *archangel* implies that he is the "leader or commander of angels" and is perfectly consistent with the word translated "shout." The word *shout* is the original word *keleusma,* which means "a command or order." Perhaps the order or command here is the same one that John heard in Revelation 4:1: "Come up hither."

4. The "dead in Christ" will rise from their graves and other places where they lie

When a believer in Jesus Christ passes away, his soul goes to be with Christ (2 Cor. 5:6-8), but the physical body is usually buried or cremated. Others may have tragically died at sea or in some other way in which the body was never recovered for proper burial. Regardless of where or in what state the body is at the time of the rapture, Christ will raise it up, recreate it, and reunite it to the soul of the saint of God to which it belonged. There is no reason to believe that these being raised are only New Testament believers; this resurrection likely includes all Old Testament believers as well.

Death and its consequences to the human body is the ultimate proof that our flesh is both mortal and corruptible. However, according to the 1 Corinthian passage, at the resurrection, the corruptible body takes on incorruption and mortality takes on immortality. What a glorious thought this is! Paul used words like this to describe it: "Death is swallowed up in victory," and "O death, where is thy sting? O grave, where is thy victory?" (I Cor. 15:54-55).

Paul's immediate purpose in the 1 Thessalonians passage is to assure believers concerning their loved ones who were also believers but had already passed away. He wanted them to know that their having died did not mean they would not have a part in the rapture. He closes the section by saying, "Wherefore comfort one another with these words" (1 Thess. 4:18). No greater comfort can be given to grieving loved ones than to let them know that God says that there is hope beyond the grave and reunion beyond this earth.

5. Living believers will vanish from the earth

In both of these passages, we see the instantaneous nature of the rapture. In 1 Thessalonians 4:17, Paul says that we will be "caught up together." He uses the word *harpazo,* which means "to snatch out or away." In 1 Corinthians 15:52 he says that it will happen "In a moment, in the twinkling of an eye."

Someone has humorously said that "the *twinkle of an eye* is the time it takes for the light to turn green and the lady behind you to start honking." Both passages let us know that the rapture will happen very quickly. It will literally be a now-you–see-me, now-you-don't event.

There will be no time to take anything with you, but there is nothing down here that you will need up there.

Likely, the clothes you will be wearing will simply fall to the earth in a heap as the body is taken right out of them. Have no fear, however, because immediately we will be wearing sparkling white robes of righteousness issued by our divine designer, Jesus Christ.

6. The bodies of both the living and the dead will be changed into that which is glorified

Changing the human body is, in our day, a multi-billion dollar industry. These modifications include diets, exercise programs, and surgical procedures. While nothing is wrong with these, at best they allow us to lose a few pounds, strengthen a few muscles, feel better, and hopefully look a little better to everyone else.

Instead of the struggles we must endure to accomplish what we wish for our physical bodies down here, the rapture will bring about change that is complete, immediate, and eternal.

The word *change* in 1 Corinthians 15:51 is the original word *allasso*, which means "to exchange one thing for another or transform." Our mortal, fleshly, and corruptible bodies will be "transformed" into what we call a "glorified body." Scripture does not give all the details of what that will be like, but we do have a glorious hint:

Beloved, now are we the sons of God, and it doth not yet appear what we shall be: but we know that, when he shall appear, we shall be like him; for we shall see him as he is. (1 John 3:2)

The "him" that John refers to is Jesus Christ. The words "as he is," present tense, refer to Him in His resurrected and glorified body. We will be like Him! The few accounts of Jesus' appearing after His resurrection and before His ascension note His glorified condition:

- He walked
- He could be seen
- He spoke and could be heard
- He could be touched
- He was able to break bread and eat
- He was able to disappear and reappear at a different location
- He was not bound by gravity … He ascended

The Apostle Paul also points to this dramatic, glorious change in other places:

For our conversation is in heaven; from whence also we look for the Saviour, the Lord Jesus Christ: Who shall change our vile body, that it may be fashioned like unto his glorious body, according to the working whereby he is able even to subdue all things unto himself. (Phil. 3:20-21)

So also *is* the resurrection of the dead. It is sown in corruption; it is raised in incorruption: It is sown in dishonour; it is raised in glory: it is sown in weakness; it is raised in power: It is sown a natural body; it is raised a spiritual body. There is a natural body, and there is a spiritual body. And so it is written, The first man Adam was made a living soul; the last Adam *was made* a quickening spirit. Howbeit that *was* not first which is spiritual, but that which is natural; and afterward that which is spiritual. The first man *is* of the earth, earthy: the second man *is* the Lord from heaven. As *is* the earthy, such *are* they also that are earthy: and as *is* the heavenly, such *are* they also that are heavenly. And as we have borne the image of the earthy, we shall also bear the image of the heavenly. (1 Cor. 15:42-49)

Because our bodies will be incorruptible, neither sickness, disease, aging, pain, nor even death can be remotely possible. It is no wonder that John would pray, "Even so, come Lord Jesus."

7. In glorified bodies, the saints meet Jesus in the air and return to Heaven with Him

Perhaps no greater, sweeter, precious, and assuring words in the Bible are "so shall we ever be with the Lord" (1 Thess. 4:17). If we are with Jesus, **all is well**; no matter what will be happening on earth, **all is well**;

regardless of what we have suffered in the past, **all is well**. This is why the coming of Jesus is for the believer our blessed hope!

Left after the Rapture

In America, the majority of the population claim to be Christian, and we certainly hope that they are. One can imagine the great vacancies created when every believer is suddenly taken out of mainstream activity. Millions will be taken from the job market; homes will be left vacant; automobiles will sit abandoned; from elementary to college, school enrollments will be depleted; every area of life as we know it will be immediately changed for those who are left behind. The logistics of continuing operations at every level of life will be incredibly complicated.

Remember, however, that the rapture affects more than America, it is global. Every country where believers live will face the issues that vast numbers of absences create, which will be a game changer for international diplomatic relations. Many countries now dominated by other religions will suddenly become superior in population and power to those which are currently Christian-majority nations. Think of the ramifications of Islamic, Buddhist, and Hindu nations alone if they do not have to concern themselves with Christian nations. The rapture sets the stage and opens the door for all that God has said about Tribulation Period events.

Paul's primary theme for both letters he wrote to the Thessalonians was the Second Coming of Christ. The second chapter of his second letter is particularly informative regarding earthly conditions after the rapture, described as follows:

1. All spiritual influence has been removed

    > For the mystery of iniquity doth already work: only he who now letteth will let, until he be taken out of the way. *(2 Thess. 2:7)*

    The King James English words *letteth* and *let* mean "to restrain." God's restraining force in our world today is the Holy Spirit. Paul uses the masculine pronoun *he* to refer to the work of the Holy Spirit, who holds back much of the evil that could exist in our present world.

    At the salvation experience, the Holy Spirit of God takes up residency in the body of the new believer. The believer's body becomes the "temple of the Holy Ghost, which is in you" (1 Cor. 6:19) and remains there until death or the rapture. The Holy Spirit works not only to comfort, guide, seal, and instruct the believer, but He also protects him from many evil forces of which that believer may never be aware. Satan and his forces can do nothing to the child of God without going through Him first.

    Without a doubt, much evil exists in our country today. However, because of the restraining work of the Holy Spirit, not as much evil exists as there could be. Traveling to countries where the Gospel has not been preached magnifies the benefit of this in our nation.

In lands that do not know God, much more demonic activity, violence, and every other kind of evil occurs.

At the rapture, believers are taken out, and thus the Holy Spirit will no longer be restraining the evil that is present but has not been allowed to have free reign.

2. The Antichrist will be revealed

> Let no man deceive you by any means: for that day shall not come, except there come a falling away first, and that man of sin be revealed, the son of perdition (2 Thess. 2:3)

> And then shall that Wicked be revealed, whom the Lord shall consume with the spirit of his mouth, and shall destroy with the brightness of his coming: Even him, whose coming is after the working of Satan with all power and signs and lying wonders (2 Thess. 2:8-9)

An expanded look at the person of the Antichrist is addressed in chapter 2. However, here Paul makes it clear that the Antichrist will not be revealed until the Holy Spirit is "taken out of the way" … the rapture.

If indeed our generation will be yet alive at the rapture, then the Antichrist may well be present with us today. Though many have speculated about who he is, using personalities that have come on the scene of human history, such speculation is unnecessary and futile in most cases. Trying to name the Antichrist will likely prove to be embarrassing to the one who is naming him as well as to Christianity as a whole. God knows who he is, and we do well to leave that to Him.

3. The fate is sealed for those who have rejected Christ

> And with all deceivableness of unrighteousness in them that perish; because they received not the love of the truth, that they might be saved. And for this cause God shall send them strong delusion, that they should believe a lie: That they all might be damned who believed not the truth, but had pleasure in unrighteousness. (2 Thess. 2:10-12)

Jesus Christ commissions the child of God to take the Gospel to "every creature." Reaching lost souls is the business of the believer. In carrying out this commission, it is always disappointing to have people reject the good news of the Gospel, choosing rather to remain in sin and take their chances on their own. Even more important than the disappointment of the witness for Christ, such a decision can be tragic for the one who rejects.

This passage clarifies that those who *"received not the love of the truth"* will not be saved after the rapture but instead will be sent a God-given *"strong delusion"* and *"believe a lie"* and be *"damned"* or condemned (emphasis added). We need not speculate what this delusion will be, but rest assured it will be sent.

Some may argue that this is not fair. On the contrary, an opportunity to be saved—even if it is offered only once—is to be seized and Christ accepted or the consequence of rejection can be expected. Look at the entire context of what is probably the most well known verse of the Bible. Jesus said:

> For God so loved the world, that he gave his only begotten Son, that whosoever believeth in him should not perish, but have everlasting life. For God sent not his Son into the world to condemn the world; but that the world through him might be saved. He that believeth on him is not condemned: but he that believeth not is condemned already, because he hath not believed in the name of the only begotten Son of God. And this is the condemnation, that light is come into the world, and men loved darkness rather than light, because their deeds were evil. For every one that doeth evil hateth the light, neither cometh to the light, lest his deeds should be reproved. But he that doeth truth cometh to the light, that his deeds may be made manifest, that they are wrought in God. (John 3:16-21)

Paul emphatically announces that the opportunity to be saved is not to be taken lightly but to be seized and accepted:

> We then, *as* workers together *with him*, beseech *you* also that ye receive not the grace of God in vain. (For he saith, I have heard thee in a time accepted, and in the day of salvation have I succoured thee:

behold, now *is* the accepted time; behold, now *is* the day of salvation.) (2 Cor. 6:1-2)

Knowing the rapture seals the fate of those who reject Christ, His free gift of salvation should have a two-fold affect: 1) For the unsaved, be saved today, before it is eternally too late; and 2) For the saved, be a persistent witness for Christ, never giving up on those we are trying to reach with the Gospel.

Throughout human history, the God-rejecting world has wanted to be without the interference of the things of God. Many have not wanted Him or have thought that they do not need Him. Following the rapture, they are going to get their wish ... or so they will think. They will try their best for seven years to bring about their own systems of government and religion. They will endeavor to have their own god and give him their allegiance and worship. Ultimately, however, they will realize that God cannot be controlled or defeated. There will be a final realization that Jesus Christ has been, is, and forever shall be the King of Kings and Lord of Lords.

CHAPTER 2

The Tribulation – part one

The supernatural nature of the events included in The Tribulation Period has caused many to doubt the validity or possibility of such things to occur. I readily admit that the things we are about to see are indeed hard to wrap our minds around. However, I want us to be reminded of these important truths:

- Information about and warnings of these events are given to us in the divinely inspired Word of God. Equally, other such events are recorded in scripture that are hard to explain. For instance, the creation event as recorded in Genesis chapters 1 and 2 gives us a vivid demonstration of God's supernatural ability. While we cannot explain how God could create all things from nothing, we believe that He did and thus we have our existence today as proof. As Bible believers, we ascribe to the fact that all scripture is TRUE and RELIABLE even if we cannot fully explain how it is executed.
- The Tribulation Period is an unveiling of the age-old spiritual battle that exists between the powers of Satan and the Superior powers of Jesus Christ. For these seven years of tribulation, the battle moves from the current invisible and spiritual world to a visible and physical conflict and ultimate finale.

- The issue of this final struggle is pointed to throughout the whole Bible, Old and New Testament alike. A singular mention in the Bible of any given subject makes that subject important. However, if the subject is continually repeated and especially if it is addressed in more than one book, we should pay special attention to it.
- In summary, God is a supernatural God; the Bible is a supernatural book; if God through His Word shows us "what will be," it makes little difference whether we think it is possible or not … It Shall Be!

Following the rapture of the saints, life on earth will change in epidemic proportions. For the next seven years, there will be tribulation in the world as Satan is given a greater liberty than was allowed while the saints and Holy Spirit restrained much of the evil until then.

Jesus, in His Olivet Discourse, gives us this description concerning the time period we are looking at and sets the stage for the next few chapters you will be reading.

> For then shall be great tribulation, such as was not since the beginning of the world to this time, no, nor ever shall be. (Mat. 24:21)

His statement is noteworthy when we consider the many local and global conflicts that have occurred through history. Jesus says that the Tribulation Period will surpass any and all that have ever happened in intensity and ramifications. History is filled with atrocities and horrific events that resulted in loss of life through war, natural disaster, unexplainable mysteries, famine, political upheaval, and the list goes on. The worst is yet to come!

As mentioned previously, there are both Old and New Testament references to the Tribulation Period. The following is a list of references and titles used for this period (emphases added):

1. *The Day of the Lord (Isa. 2:12)*
2. *The Indignation (Isa. 26:20; 34:2)*
3. *The Day of God's Vengeance (Isa. 34:8; 63:1-6)*
4. *The Time of Jacob's Trouble (Jer. 30:7)*
5. *The Seventieth Week (Dan. 9:24-27)*
6. *The Time of the End (Dan. 12:9)*
7. *The Time of Trouble such as Never Was (Dan. 12:1)*
8. *The End of This World (Mat. 13:40; 49)*
9. *The Great Day of His Wrath (Rev. 6:17)*
10. *The Hour of His Judgment (Rev. 14:7)*

In this section, we will be looking at the personalities and powers that will be predominate during these seven years. In *The Tribulation – part two*, we will be looking at the judgments God sends upon the earth, but here we need to establish the environment into which they come.

The Tribulation Period is divided into two distinctive parts. The first three and one-half years following the rapture will be seemingly peaceful as certain political and religious powers take their places. Some atrocities will likely occur, but these will be merely the brewing of the storm to come. In the last three and one-half years, absolute devastation and chaos will reign on earth. This period is often referred to as *The Great Tribulation* and is likely the period that Jesus was speaking of in the Matthew 24:21 passage quoted previously.

The Antichrist

Without a doubt, the most notable personality on earth during the Tribulation Period will be the one who is called the Antichrist. The Apostle John (same as the human writer of The Revelation) points out that there are "many antichrists" (1 John 2:18). The context of this passage makes it clear that he is referring to those, plural, who oppose Christ and have gone out from us. This references the apostasy that was already happening in John's day. However, the Antichrist of the Tribulation is one individual, singular, who will be the epitome of all those antichrists who have preceded him. He is given the name "the beast" in the book of The Revelation.

Note the following information concerning the Antichrist:

1. He will be revealed soon after the rapture

> Let no man deceive you by any means: for that day shall not come, except there come a falling away first, and that man of sin be revealed, the son of perdition; Who opposeth and exalteth himself above all that is called God, or that is worshipped; so that he as God sitteth in the temple of God, shewing himself that he is God. Remember ye not, that, when I was yet with you, I told you these things? And now ye know what withholdeth that

he might be revealed in his time. For the mystery of iniquity doth already work: only he who now letteth will let, until he be taken out of the way. And then shall that Wicked be revealed, whom the Lord shall consume with the spirit of his mouth, and shall destroy with the brightness of his coming: Even him, whose coming is after the working of Satan with all power and signs and lying wonders, And with all deceivableness of unrighteousness in them that perish; because they received not the love of the truth, that they might be saved. (2 Thess. 2:3-10)

History is full of individuals who were thought to be this one called the Antichrist. Such speculation and labeling is unnecessary and quite embarrassing when that certain individual, along with his accusers, pass from human history. However, if God's designed date for the rapture is in the near future, then this individual, the Antichrist, could very well be present among us today. Again, venturing to identify him would be an unwise thing to do.

Because of the persecution the believers in Thessalonica were experiencing, many thought that the rapture had already taken place and they were then in the Tribulation. Paul is writing to correct their error, and he assures them by stating the elements that will be true when the Tribulation does come. The words of verse 3, "that day," are a reference to the Tribulation.

- There will be an apostasy … a great falling away (vs. 3)
- The Antichrist will be revealed … "man of sin" (vs. 3), "that Wicked" (vs. 8)
- The Holy Spirit will be removed … at the rapture (vs. 6)

2. He will be empowered by Satan

The Antichrist will be a living, breathing human being. However, he will be possessed by and empowered by Satan. With this satanic power, he will have great influence, be a great deceiver, perform miracles, and have the forces of demonic beings as an ally.

John gives us a rather lengthy and vivid description of the Antichrist and his source of power in Revelation chapter 13.

> And I stood upon the sand of the sea, and saw a beast rise up out of the sea, having seven heads and ten horns, and upon his horns ten crowns, and upon his heads the name of blasphemy. And the beast which I saw was like unto a leopard, and his feet were as the feet of a bear, and his mouth as the mouth of a lion: and **the dragon gave him his power, and his seat, and great authority.** And I saw one of his heads as it were wounded to death; and his deadly wound was healed: and all the world

wondered after the beast. And they worshipped the dragon which gave power unto the beast: and they worshipped the beast, saying, Who is like unto the beast? who is able to make war with him? And there was given unto him a mouth speaking great things and blasphemies; and power was given unto him to continue forty and two months. And he opened his mouth in blasphemy against God, to blaspheme his name, and his tabernacle, and them that dwell in heaven. (Rev. 13:1-6, emphasis added)

Notice first that the Antichrist is said to "rise up out of the sea." Most theologians believe that the metaphor of the sea is speaking of the Gentile nations. If this is indeed the case, then he could rise from any place on the globe, other than Israel. He could be Arab, Oriental, European, or from any other Gentile nation, even America.

Secondly, his power comes from "the dragon." The identity of the dragon is given to us in Revelation 12:9 – "And the great dragon was cast out, that old serpent, called the Devil, and Satan, which decieveth the whole world." While Satan is not sovereign or omnipotent, he is indeed a powerful foe to be reckoned with. In this passage, we are told that Satan gets what he has always desired most ... worship. Satan's human instrument, the beast or Antichrist, is also worshipped and deemed invincible.

Finally, he speaks blasphemy against God and everything about God. This should not be surprising since his power is from Satan. More than a glimpse of what is actually happening, this is the forces of Satan in conflict with the forces of Jesus Christ. The root of all the chaos that happens in the Tribulation is that Satan is doing his best to defeat God and all that pertains to Him. His pawn, the Antichrist, will have great success in leading the unbelieving world in this all-out-attack on God, by the power that he has been endowed with.

Did you notice, however, that the power he has been given is limited? It is limited by God's decree! He, the Antichrist, is given "forty and two months" or three and one-half years ... he and his god Satan have a rude awakening coming at the end of these seven years.

3. He will come as an imitation of Christ

Satan has always been and will continue to be the master counterfeiter. He tries in every way possible to imitate God and His work because what he earnestly desires is to be God. At the very opening of the Tribulation, we see Satan continuing his work of imitating.

> And I saw, and behold a white horse: and he that sat on him had a bow; and a crown was given unto him: and he went forth conquering, and to conquer. (Rev. 6:2)

At a casual glance, this verse might appear to speak about Jesus Christ. However, as we look deeper, we find that this is not Christ but Antichrist … another counterfeit offering of Satan. We look more closely at this verse in the next chapter, but may I point out the fake identity of the one spoken of here:

- He is riding on a white horse – Jesus returns at the battle of Armageddon on a white horse (Rev. 19:11)
- His horse is white, a symbol of peace, though it is a false peace – Jesus is the "Prince of Peace"
- He has a bow … notice, however, that there is no mention of arrows … his power is deceptive – Jesus returns with a sword … true power … His Word (Rev. 19:15)
- He has a crown … however, the word for crown here is *stephenos* or "victor's crown" – Jesus returns with a crown … his is called *diadema* or "Kingly crown" (Rev. 19:12)
- He goes forth "conquering, and to conquer" … and conquer he will for a short period – Jesus will not be "trying to conquer," He will Triumph as Conqueror

4. He will oppose all that has to do with God

We have seen already in the Revelation 13 passage that the Antichrist will speak blasphemies against God. Daniel also prophesied this over five hundred years before the first coming of Christ.

And he shall speak great words against the most
High, and shall wear out the saints of the most
High, and think to change times and laws: and
they shall be given into his hand until a time and
times and the dividing of time. (Dan. 7:25)

The "he" in this verse is the beast that has been
identified as the Antichrist. He will wage war
against those who come to faith in Christ during the
Tribulation Period; he will make laws that fit his own
needs; but notice again that his time is limited. The
phrase "time and times and the dividing of time" no
doubt references a period of three and one-half years
(time – 1; times – 2; dividing of times – ½).

And the king shall do according to his will; and he
shall exalt himself, and magnify himself above every
god, and shall speak marvellous things against the
God of gods, and shall prosper till the indignation
be accomplished: for that that is determined shall
be done. (Dan. 11:36)

The "king" Daniel refers to is the Antichrist.
What Daniel prophesies here comes to pass during
the Tribulation as the Antichrist sets himself up to
be worshipped as a god. His success will last only as
long as this period of "the indignation," a reference
to the Tribulation, endures. This period will "be
accomplished" and what God has already determined
shall be done!

5. He will rally the nations around himself

Even in our present world, all the nations are looking for someone who has the answers to the world's problems of lack of peace, economics, and unity among the nations. Through satanic influence, the Antichrist will come on to the scene with what the world thinks to be exactly what they have been looking for. He achieves what no man in recent history has achieved … global leadership.

> And in the latter time of their kingdom, when the transgressors are come to the full, a king of fierce countenance, and understanding dark sentences, shall stand up. And his power shall be mighty, but not by his own power: and he shall destroy wonderfully, and shall prosper, and practise, and shall destroy the mighty and the holy people. And through his policy also he shall cause craft to prosper in his hand; and he shall magnify himself in his heart, and by peace shall destroy many: he shall also stand up against the Prince of princes; but he shall be broken without hand. (Dan. 8:23-25)

The "king" is, here again, the one that is to come, the Antichrist. Daniel describes his means of operation:

- He is mystical
- He is powerful, but not by his own power … we learned earlier that his power comes from Satan
- He is blatantly opposed to God and His people

- He is shrewd at business … "cause craft to prosper in his hand"
- He rules empirically
- He uses the disguise of peace to make it happen

Daniel also lets us know that he will meet his match when he comes up against the Prince of princes who is Jesus Christ – Revelation 19:11-16.

6. He will establish a peace treaty with Israel and then break it

The most intriguing nation in all of the world's history is the nation of Israel. God, in His sovereignty, chose to bring the nation of Israel into being through Abraham, Isaac, and Jacob and then put His own name on that people. Make no mistake about it, the Jewish people are God's chosen people.

The most tragic mistake that the nation of Israel ever made was the rejection of God Incarnate, Jesus Christ. Even though they were looking for the appearing of Messiah, they willfully rejected Him when He came. The result was, except for a remnant who have believed (Rom. 11:5), the nation of Israel was given a "spirit of slumber" concerning spiritual things.

What then? Israel hath not obtained that which he seeketh for; but the election hath obtained it, and the rest were blinded (According as it is written, God hath given them the spirit of slumber, eyes that they should not see, and ears that they should not hear;) unto this day. (Rom. 11:7-8)

There is wonderful news, however, concerning the future of Israel. The Jewish people will come to true faith in Christ, likely in the first half of the Tribulation Period.

And so all Israel shall be saved: as it is written, There shall come out of Sion the Deliverer, and shall turn away ungodliness from Jacob: For this *is* my covenant unto them, when I shall take away their sins. As concerning the gospel, *they are* enemies for your sakes: but as touching the election, *they are* beloved for the fathers' sakes. (Rom. 11:26-28)

Much more could be written concerning God's dealings with Israel, but suffice it to say, God is not finished with this nation. As mentioned in the first chapter of this book, Israel is front-and-center when it comes to the prophetic message of the last days. With Israel now back in her land and once again recognized as an autonomous nation, all prophecies concerning her are now ready to be fulfilled.

Today, Israel, along with the United States, is the burr under the saddle of many nations in our world. National leaders have yet to figure out what can be done to resolve this complicated issue.

However, when the Antichrist enters the scene, he will have the apparent solution to the problem. What that solution is, is unknown at this time though we do know that it is a part of biblical prophecy. We refer again to the prophecies of Daniel:

> And he shall confirm the covenant with many for one week: and in the midst of the week he shall cause the sacrifice and the oblation to cease, and for the overspreading of abominations he shall make it desolate, even until the consummation, and that determined shall be poured upon the desolate. (Dan. 9:27)

Theologians generally agree that "week" here is used to refer to "a week of years" or a period of seven years. The "he" is again speaking of the Antichrist that is to come, who is said to make a covenant with Israel for seven years. However, "in the midst of the week" or halfway through the seven years (3 ½ years), he will break that covenant. Israel then becomes the archenemy of the Antichrist and his global powers for the remainder of the seven-year period. Perhaps the reason for this breach of the agreement is the nation of Israel as a whole is coming to true faith in God. This would put the satanically empowered Antichrist at eternal odds with the people of Israel.

7. He will be killed and have a resurrection

At least twice, the book of The Revelation references a miraculous death and resurrection of the beast. This event seems to be the deciding factor for the nations' rallying behind the leadership of the Antichrist.

> And I saw one of his heads as it were wounded to death; and his deadly wound was healed: and all the world wondered after the beast. And they worshipped the dragon which gave power unto the beast: and they worshipped the beast, saying, Who is like unto the beast? who is able to make war with him? (Rev. 13:3-4)

Again, we see Satan as the master counterfeiter in his attempt to gain the following of the world. The One and Only True God did indeed die, was buried, and rose again! This is Satan's ploy to "be like the most High."

> How art thou fallen from heaven, O Lucifer, son of the morning! *how* art thou cut down to the ground, which didst weaken the nations! For thou hast said in thine heart, I will ascend into heaven, I will exalt my throne above the stars of God: I will sit also upon the mount of the congregation, in the sides of the north: I will ascend above the heights of the clouds; I will be like the most High. (Isa. 14:12-14)

God's declaration did not stop there, however. He goes on to declare Satan's end in the verses that follow:

> Yet thou shalt be brought down to hell, to the sides of the pit. They that see thee shall narrowly look

upon thee, *and* consider thee, *saying, Is* this the man that made the earth to tremble, that did shake kingdoms; *That* made the world as a wilderness, and destroyed the cities thereof; *that* opened not the house of his prisoners? All the kings of the nations, *even* all of them, lie in glory, every one in his own house. But thou art cast out of thy grave like an abominable branch, *and as* the raiment of those that are slain, thrust through with a sword, that go down to the stones of the pit; as a carcase trodden under feet. Thou shalt not be joined with them in burial, because thou hast destroyed thy land, *and* slain thy people: the seed of evildoers shall never be renowned. Prepare slaughter for his children for the iniquity of their fathers; that they do not rise, nor possess the land, nor fill the face of the world with cities. For I will rise up against them, saith the LORD of hosts, and cut off from Babylon the name, and remnant, and son, and nephew, saith the LORD. I will also make it a possession for the bittern, and pools of water: and I will sweep it with the besom of destruction, saith the LORD of hosts. The LORD of hosts hath sworn, saying, Surely as I have thought, so shall it come to pass; and as I have purposed, *so* shall it stand (Isa. 14:15-24)

The unbelieving world will swoon at this remarkable man who has such miraculous power. They will give him and his god, Satan, worship and allegiance in all that he commands to be done:

> The beast that thou sawest was, and is not; and shall ascend out of the bottomless pit, and go into perdition: ***and they that dwell on the earth shall wonder***, whose names were not written in the book of life from the foundation of the world, when they behold the beast that was, and is not, and yet is. (Rev. 17:8, emphasis added)

I must confess that I cannot be dogmatic as to whether this resurrection is indeed a satanic miracle where the individual truly died and was brought back to life or if it was a cleverly designed deception that made people believe that it actually happened. I am certain that it accomplishes what it was intended to do, which is make the unbelieving world follow after this satanically empowered fraud.

8. He will dominate the earth until he is crushed by Jesus Christ at the battle of Armageddon.

    This event is described in Revelation 19:11-21 and is covered in its entirety in chapter four of this book.

9. He will be the first to be cast into the lake of fire

    It is a great thing to know how the story will end. In spite of the dominance that the Antichrist has exercised, the power that he has wielded, the following that he has acquired, the adoration that he has experienced, and the name that he has made for himself, he is no match for Jehovah God. His reign will come to an abrupt end and his eternal destiny is sealed.

> And the beast was taken, and with him the false prophet that wrought miracles before him, with which he deceived them that had received the mark of the beast, and them that worshipped his image. These both were cast alive into a lake of fire burning with brimstone. (Rev. 19:20)

Notice the wording in this verse: *"These were cast alive into the lake of fire burning with brimstone"* (emphasis added). Did you notice the word *alive*? Evidently, both the beast and the false prophet survive the battle of Armageddon, but they do not escape … they are cast "alive" into the lake of fire.

The One-World Religion

A commonly asked question in our world today is, "Why are there so many different religions?" The simple answer is that for everything that God has created to be **true**, Satan has counterfeited with that which is **false**. In spite of the widely accepted notion that "all religions are the same," the truth is, they are not. The Bible and the truth contained in it remain to be the one and only source of God's divine revelation to man in our present age.

Once the rapture has occurred and true believers have been taken from the world, the opportunity to establish a single religious system that will encompass all the nations will arise. The gospel will be preached during the Tribulation, and many will be truly converted by that message. However, the individual costs of believing will be extreme because of the persecution resulting from their faith.

This religious system, the "One-World Church," is referred to in Revelation 17:5 as being "MYSTERY BABYLON THE GREAT, THE MOTHER OF HARLOTS AND ABOMINATIONS OF THE EARTH." This "church," in the symbolic language common to the book of Revelation, is referred to as a "woman" or more descriptively as "the harlot." Since Satan is the one behind the establishment and progress of this religion, we should not be surprised by the horrific description that we have of it in scripture:

> And there came one of the seven angels which had the seven vials, and talked with me, saying unto me, Come hither; I will shew unto thee the judgment of the great whore that sitteth upon many waters: With whom the kings of the earth have committed fornication, and the inhabitants of the earth have been made drunk with the wine of her fornication. So he carried me away in the spirit into the wilderness: and I saw a woman sit upon a scarlet coloured beast, full of names of blasphemy, having seven heads and ten horns. And the woman was arrayed in purple and scarlet colour, and decked with gold and precious stones and pearls, having a

golden cup in her hand full of abominations and
filthiness of her fornication (Rev. 17:1-4)

Significantly, this religious movement is identified with
and titled "MYSTERY BABYLON." The root of the term
Babylon extends back to the book of Genesis chapters 10 and
11, covering the events of the building of the Tower of Babel.
In these chapters, the nations are attempting to build a tower
that would reach heaven, allowing them to reach God by
their own human effort and unifying all nations in this single
religious endeavor. God, however, confounds their language
and disperses them throughout the regions.

Various passages in scripture clearly use the term "Babylon"
for a great system of religious error, a counterfeit or pseudo
religion that plagued Israel in the Old Testament and gave
birth to various sects found in the New Testament as well.
Interestingly, the Old Testament city of Babylon is mentioned
more times in the Bible (260 times) than any other city other
than Jerusalem. Satan has always been active in the area of
false religions, and *Babylon* is the biblical name given to his
enterprise.

The aged Apostle John is given a view of this system as
recorded in Revelation 17 (quoted above). Using metaphoric
and symbolic language, he gives us vital information about
this religious system that will dominate the globe during the
Tribulation. Occasionally, he gives us the meaning behind the
symbols that he uses, which enhances our understanding of
this satanic work and provides indicators that help us identify
connections with groups in the 21st century.

Note these things about "The Harlot" as seen in Revelation 17:

1. She sits on seven mountains

    In John's vision of the "woman," he notes that she is sitting on a "beast" that has "seven heads and ten horns." Such language would be dubious at best and leave us wondering "What in world does this mean?" were it not for the explanation that he gives in the verses that follow:

    And here is the mind which hath wisdom. The seven heads are seven mountains, in which the woman sitteth. (Rev. 17:9)

    This verse gives us insight into the "One-World Church." The woman sitting on the seven mountains is doubtlessly pointing out the geographic location from which the "church" will operate ... its headquarters. The city of Rome is known as The City of Seven Hills, giving us a strong indication that this One-World Church, MYSTERY BABYLON, will be headquartered in Rome. For many centuries, Rome has been known for its religious affiliations, namely the Roman Catholic religion.

2. She is regally attired

    John's description of the way she is "arrayed" in verse 4 is also an important identification. Her robes are purple and scarlet; she is decked with gold; she is wearing precious stones and pearls; she has a cup in her hand. This description is all too familiar with the trappings of the ecclesiastical pomp of today's high officials of the Roman Catholic and Greek Orthodox churches.

Also noteworthy, the word *catholic* means "universal."

The evidence is strong that this One-World Church, MYSTERY BABYLON, will be a revived Roman Empire, composed of all the world religions, including Islam, Buddhism, Hinduism, and the rest, under the auspices of the Roman Catholic Church. Occasionally we see news articles that report consolidation efforts already being attempted. With Christian influence taken out of the way at the rapture and Satan given a liberty that is presently restrained, the unifying of world religions could be accomplished rather quickly.

3. The kings of the earth have united with her

Remember that the beast upon which the "woman" is sitting (vs. 4) has "seven heads" (defined as mountains in vs. 9) and "ten horns." The same chapter defines these "ten horns."

And the ten horns which thou sawest are ten kings, which have received no kingdom as yet; but receive power as kings one hour with the beast. (Rev. 17:12)

These will likely be ten newly appointed kings, appointed by the dictator, the Antichrist, and these ten kings will immediately submit themselves and their individual nations to the authority of the Antichrist. In so doing, they will also submit their nations to the state church that has been established.

> With whom the kings of the earth have committed fornication, and the inhabitants of the earth have been made drunk with the wine of her fornication. (Rev. 17:2)

The word "fornication" here speaks about spiritual adultery or unity. The efforts of the "church" and the politics of the nations will unify to create one massive power.

4. She is a persecutor of true believers

History is replete with instances of persecution under the name of religion. The greatest persecution is yet to come by means of the One-World Church and the authority of the Antichrist with his global allies.

People will come to true faith in Christ during the Tribulation, including both those who have not had an opportunity to believe before the rapture as well as the Jewish people spoken of earlier. Combined, these are the "saints" spoken of in Revelation 17:6:

> And I saw the woman drunken with the blood of the saints, and with the blood of the martyrs of

Jesus: and when I saw her, I wondered with great admiration. (Rev. 17:6)

From time to time individuals say, "If I see that the rapture has happened and all the Christians are gone, then I will get saved ... but not until then." The truth is, no they won't! First, they will be deceived into believing a lie (mentioned in the first chapter) and, secondly, if that individual will not be saved now when it costs him nothing, why would he be saved in the Tribulation when it will likely cost him his life?

5. Ultimately, the kings of the earth, under the direction of the Antichrist, will turn on her and destroy her

Satan is never satisfied! The One-World Church will have been established and all nations of the earth will be submitted to her. However, Satan wants exclusive rights to worship and that it be him alone who is worshipped. We will see more about this a little later. To make way for the Satan worship that is come, the "harlot" must be destroyed:

And the ten horns which thou sawest upon the beast, these shall hate the whore, and shall make her desolate and naked, and shall eat her flesh, and burn her with fire. For God hath put in their hearts to fulfil his will, and to agree, and give their kingdom unto the beast, until the words of God shall be fulfilled. And the woman which thou sawest is that great city, which reigneth over the kings of the earth. (Rev. 17:16-18)

The duration of the "church" is unknown. We do know that it will come about sometime after the rapture and will end sometime before the end of the Tribulation. Perhaps the reign will last four to five years.

The One-World Government

The desire of some for world domination has always been present. In early world history, a number have even been successful in their quest and have achieved global power. Many others have tried and failed. Some in our day wish for it; for instance, the radical Muslim movements that are ever seeking national takeovers in their quest for global domination. During the Tribulation, the Antichrist will try and will succeed in becoming the one global power.

Immediately following the rapture, the Antichrist will step onto the scene, or if he is already on the political scene, he will rise quickly to a position of supreme power and authority. He will be energized by satanic power and through his use of deception, fear tactics, and an offer of global peace and unity, he will become the object of the world's affection. Scripture does not give us all of the details about how he rises to this position, but the deciding influencing factor for the world was his resurrection from the dead.

In Revelation 17, John is given the chronological order of those who have, are, and will hold global power:

> And there are seven kings: five are fallen, and one is, and the other is not yet come; and when he cometh, he must continue a short space. (Rev. 17:10)

John is told that the total number of global empires is seven. At the time John was writing this, under the inspiration of the Holy Spirit, five of these empires have fallen, one is, one is yet to come, and this final one will be brief. Historically broken down, the list would look like this:

- Past, "are fallen" – Egypt, Assyria, Babylon, Persia, and Greece
- Present in John's day, "is" – Rome
- Future, "yet to come" – The Beast or Antichrist

On a positive note, another global empire will not exist on earth until the arrival of the Antichrist during the Tribulation Period.

> And the beast that was, and is not, even he is the eighth, and is of the seven, and goeth into perdition. And the ten horns which thou sawest are ten kings, which have received no kingdom as yet; but receive power as kings one hour with the beast. These have one mind, and shall give their power and strength unto the beast. These shall make war with the Lamb, and the Lamb shall overcome them: for he is Lord of lords, and King of kings: and they that

are with him are called, and chosen, and faithful. (Rev. 17:11-14)

The Antichrist is not only the seventh on the list of global empires, but he is also the eighth as well … probably because of his death and resurrection. He appoints ten kings over ten nations, and each of them is devoted to the Antichrist and his empirical rule. Perhaps, during this time, smaller and less powerful nations are dissolved and absorbed into these ten nations over which these ten kings reign.

This passage notably references their consolidated military power. The ultimate and final battle of this united effort is when they will confront Jesus Christ in the Battle of Armageddon (Rev. 19).

Such a united, international alliance is not that hard to imagine. On April 4, 1949, the North Atlantic Treaty Organization (NATO) formally commenced. According to NATO's website, their express purpose is *"to safeguard the freedom and security of its members through political and military means"* (NATO). This may indeed be a noble cause at the present. However, one can imagine that if the primary leaders of these nations were corrupt then there would be global repercussions. A satanic-empowered Antichrist ruling and ten Antichrist-appointed kings over the nations would no doubt corrupt. Perhaps, the framework for global power is already in place.

Various aspects of the economic issues of the One-World Government will be addressed when we look into the forced obedience of the False Prophet.

Many often ask, "What about the United States of America in relation to this Tribulation Period?" Prophetic passages of the Bible do not, in fact, mention our nation. This leaves us only to speculation about what the future holds for our people in relation to the prophetic picture. I would pose two possible scenarios; one positive, the other negative:

1. America is called a "Christian Nation" … some debate exists about the validity of this title. Perhaps, at the rapture, the major part of the American populous is taken out to be with Christ, thus leaving a relatively small population in the entire country. Such depletion could eliminate America as a world power among the remaining nations. This is certainly the most desirable proposition.
2. Possibly, America may have been either destroyed or taken over by another country when the Tribulation begins. This is a terrible but not impossible proposition.

Each of us should pray earnestly for the United States of America. Our land is in need of revival, a fresh breath from God, and a return to the Word of God and the God of the Word. Our time remaining may be very short and the need is great. PRAY!

The False Prophet

As we have learned, the one called "the beast" is the Antichrist. In Revelation chapter 13, another beast is introduced, who is also called "the False Prophet."

Satan, the master counterfeiter, once again takes that which is holy and creates that which is unholy. His counterfeit operation looks like this:

- The Dragon (Satan) – counterfeit Father
- The First Beast (Antichrist) – counterfeit Son
- The Second Beast (False Prophet) – counterfeit Holy Spirit

The False Prophet joins with the Antichrist in his unholy tirade and seems to be the one who represents the spiritual side of the duet. His purpose is to promote the causes of the Antichrist and make sure that all submission is given unto him.

The False Prophet will have three primary responsibilities:

1. Lead in the worship of the Antichrist

    The imitation of God's Holy Trinity here is plain. The Holy Spirit points us to God the Son. Here, the False Prophet points people to the Antichrist.

    And I beheld another beast coming up out of the earth; and he had two horns like a lamb, and he spake as a dragon. And he exerciseth all the power of the first beast before him, and causeth the earth and them which dwell therein to worship the first beast, whose deadly wound was healed. (Rev. 13:11-12)

As a part of this worship, an idol or image is set up in honor of the Antichrist, and all people are required to worship this image or else die. Amazingly, this False Prophet has the ability to make the image speak, by either satanic miracle or mere deception.

2. Perform miracles

To convince the world's population to submit to the Antichrist, both physically and spiritually, will require that they see the supernatural nature of him and his cohort. The miracles of Jesus during His earthly ministry caused many to believe on Him; here is an unholy attempt to do the same.

And he doeth great wonders, so that he maketh fire come down from heaven on the earth in the sight of men, And deceiveth them that dwell on the earth by the means of those miracles which he had power to do in the sight of the beast; saying to them that dwell on the earth, that they should make an image to the beast, which had the wound by a sword, and did live. (Rev. 13:13-14)

3. Force Obedience

Almost any discussion concerning the book of The Revelation and the Tribulation Period will ultimately include conversation about "the mark of the beast."

Revelation 13 discusses the work of the False Prophet that this subject:

> And he causeth all, both small and great, rich and poor, free and bond, to receive a mark in their right hand, or in their foreheads: And that no man might buy or sell, save he that had the mark, or the name of the beast, or the number of his name. Here is wisdom. Let him that hath understanding count the number of the beast: for it is the number of a man; and his number is Six hundred threescore and six. (Rev. 13:16-18)

Enforcement of the law that requires subservience to the Antichrist will mean making logistical arrangements. Since survival would depend upon the population's ability to buy and sell goods, the economy is the perfect place to enforce the law. Any and all commerce, whether a business transaction, the purchase of a home, car, or clothes, or even food to eat will require that the merchant as well as the customer be the bearer of this identifying mark showing allegiance to Antichrist.

Lest someone dismiss the possibility of such a law as being nonsense, consider all the things that you presently cannot do without the government-issued Social Security card that you carry in your wallet. Yet, we think nothing at all about using this number to secure employment, do banking, file our taxes, and so on. During the Tribulation, all control of the government is under the authority of the Antichrist and his enforcer, the False Prophet.

Consider for a moment the number itself, six-six-six. Verse 18 tells us that this is the "number of a man." The number *seven* is generally accepted as the "number of perfection." By the way, the number seven is repeated throughout the book of the Revelation ... God is still the sovereign through it all. Six is one short of seven ... man is short of perfection; he is imperfect.

As recent as a couple of decades ago, artistic renderings of the mark of the beast would present individuals with an ugly black tattoo of the numbers *666* on their foreheads or right hands. The sight was scary to say the least ... who would submit to such defamation?

However, in our age of modern technology, such cosmetic infringement would not be necessary. Microscopic chips, RFID (radio frequency identification), have been developed, originally for use with pets, where this tiny chip is inserted beneath the skin of the animal. Shot records as well as owner information is imbedded on the chip for easy identification should the pet be lost from its owner. Further development of this product has shown that entire medical records of humans could also be embedded in this kind of chip. How convenient would it be if a person were in an accident and was unconscious or away from his regular health care area, if all medical conditions and records were immediately available by scanning this chip? In October of 2004, the FDA approved the use of these microscopic chips for humans.

The benefit of such technology is seemingly endless. The medical records benefit is obvious, but what if every child born were to have a chip inserted at birth? Can location detection be included on the chip so that if the child is ever missing, through GPS technology, the whereabouts of the child can immediately be identified? Many or most adults would volunteer for the same procedure. What if bank accounts and other personal information could also be stored on the chip with constant updates through wireless computer networks? Carrying cumbersome credit cards or cash would be needless. No reasonable person of this generation would doubt that such technology is possible and even likely available for the marketplace already.

Back to the subject of the False Prophet and the mark of the beast: this kind of technology may very well be used for demarcation for qualified consumers. With a chip under the skin of every individual, all accounts and transactions could be controlled based on the data supplied by the chip. Purchases would be made by merely scanning the chip, the same way that we use UPC codes at the checkout of our grocery store. The key component of the data would be whether the individual has met the requirements set forth by the False Prophet.

This would mean a totally cashless society, but have you noticed how quickly we are moving toward this already? Please know also that I am not anti-technology when it is used for noble purposes. The use of Social Security numbers, bar codes, GPS systems, and the like is not wrong or sinful. I am merely showing that global conditions at the present will be very accommodating to the work of dubious individuals.

The One Hundred Forty-Four Thousand

As mentioned earlier, Paul has told us that the Jewish people, Israel as a whole, will come to true faith in Jesus Christ (Rom. 11). A true revival will break out in this nation. This will be, in large part, due to a very special and divine work that God will do among His people Israel by calling out some very devoted servants and messengers —one hundred and forty-four thousand of them.

> And after these things I saw four angels standing on the four corners of the earth, holding the four winds of the earth, that the wind should not blow on the earth, nor on the sea, nor on any tree. And I saw another angel ascending from the east, having the seal of the living God: and he cried with a loud voice to the four angels, to whom it was given to hurt the earth and the sea, Saying, Hurt not the earth, neither the sea, nor the trees, till we have sealed the servants of our God in their foreheads. And I heard the number of them which were sealed: *and there were* sealed an hundred *and* forty *and* four

thousand of all the tribes of the children of Israel. (Rev. 7:1-4)

Twelve thousand from each of the 12 tribes of Israel are selected and sealed by God. Their work will be the evangelizing of the nation and the world. Revelation 14 describes them as an elite group of messengers:

> And I looked, and, lo, a Lamb stood on the mount Sion, and with him an hundred forty *and* four thousand, having his Father's name written in their foreheads. And I heard a voice from heaven, as the voice of many waters, and as the voice of a great thunder: and I heard the voice of harpers harping with their harps: And they sung as it were a new song before the throne, and before the four beasts, and the elders: and no man could learn that song but the hundred *and* forty *and* four thousand, which were redeemed from the earth. These are they which were not defiled with women; for they are virgins. These are they which follow the Lamb whithersoever he goeth. These were redeemed from among men, *being* the firstfruits unto God and to the Lamb. And in their mouth was found no guile: for they are without fault before the throne of God. (Rev. 14:1-5)

These two passages of scripture eliminate the claims of the Jehovah Witnesses cult that they are the ones who make up the one hundred forty-four thousand.

The true one hundred forty-four thousand sealed and commissioned preachers of the Gospel will have huge success with multitudes coming to faith in Christ. They will likely later be martyred for their preaching, which is why John sees them standing with Christ in the Revelation 14 passages.

The Two Witnesses

In addition to the one hundred forty-four thousand Jewish witnesses, God sends two very interesting individuals into the city of Jerusalem for the last three and one-half years of the Tribulation. Revelation 11 gives us this account. The work they will do and the miracles they will perform so closely parallel the work of two Old Testament prophets that it must be more than coincidence … these prophets are Moses and Elijah.

Their ministries included the following:

- They prophesied in the streets of Jerusalem
- When anyone tried to hurt these prophets, they were killed with fire that came out of the mouths of the prophets
- They prevented rain for a period of three and one-half years
- They turned water into blood
- They had the power to smite the earth with plagues whenever they wanted

When these prophets have completed their ministry, the Antichrist is then allowed to kill them. He surely will be delighted to do so. Probably because of his contempt for these two witnesses, no burial is given to them and they lay in the streets for three and one-half days. According to verse 10, there is a great celebration at their death, so much so that they send presents to one another in celebration ... a terrible Christmas-like celebration.

For the first 1900 years after the completion of the canon of scriptures, theologians truly struggled with the information in verse 9 of this chapter.

> And they of the people and kindreds and tongues and nations shall see their dead bodies three days and an half, and shall not suffer their dead bodies to be put in graves. (Rev. 11:9)

For three and one-half days, *the whole world* sees the bodies of these witnesses lying in the street. Early theologians would wonder, "How indeed could this scene be observed by all nations?" The answer to that question is simple for us living in the 21st century. By means of television, we get regular reports from all over the world. By means of the computer and cell phone, pictures and videos can be transmitted in real time to virtually every part of the planet. Again, modern technology well accommodates the fulfillment of those things prophesied in scripture.

After three days of lying in the streets dead, God brings them back to life and they stand up. This will no doubt cause a stir on the evening news. A voice from heaven calls out, "Come up hither" and these two witnesses ascend to heaven ... the newscast just got a little more interesting. In the same hour that this happens, a great earthquake in the city kills seven thousand men of the city.

In the midst of the chaos that we have been discussing throughout this chapter, taking the time to read these fourteen verses of Revelation 11 is a great source of encouragement. They let us know that God is still in control and His power is greater than any that Satan may possess or demonstrate.

In the next chapter, we will address the series of judgments that God will pour out on earth and the wicked who are ruling it.

CHAPTER 3

The Tribulation – part two

Many misconceptions about God exist. Among these, some believe that God is only the God of love. Others hold that He is only the God of judgment. The truth is, He is perfectly both. To misunderstand or ignore this truth will cause the individual to have an erroneous faith in God and result in a tragically wrong response when it comes to a personal relationship with Him.

Speaking about the judgment of God is not very politically correct in our world. Sadly, it is also not very well received in many churches. We can often lose sight of just how sinful *sin* is in the eyes of a Holy God. For God to remain holy … which He will; for Him to abhor evil … which He does; and for Him to have a relationship with man … which He desires, sin must be judged. This is the very reason for the cross of Jesus Christ, where the payment for sin was secured and the judgment for sin was satisfied.

This reluctance to acknowledge the judgment of God might be the reason many Christians avoid reading The Revelation. To read this book, one cannot help but be confronted with the righteous judgment of God upon the wickedness of man. The judgments we are about to explore will be disconcerting to the faint-of-heart; however, the severity of these judgments, coming from the throne of God, are totally just and deserved by Satan and his followers. Not only is justice being served, but God is also cleansing the earth so that He can establish His kingdom with His people that we might reign with Him as He has always desired.

The largest section of Revelation covers this period of the Tribulation. The rapture happens at the beginning of chapter 4; the scene is heaven in chapters 4 and 5; and then the scene is primarily, not exclusively, earth for chapters 6 through 19. This latter section is where the series of God's judgments are poured out on the earth. Keep the following facts in mind as we look into this section and these judgments:

- These cover a space of seven years … the Tribulation Period
- The church is never mentioned in these chapters … it has already been taken at the rapture
- All of these judgments come from the Throne of God, where He sits as the Only True Judge
- At the center of all these events is the nation of Israel … God is bringing them back into a glorious standing with Himself
- These events will closely parallel the message of Jesus in His Olivet Discourse in Matthew 24 and 25

During this period on earth, Satan has much more liberty among men than before. He will not have complete sovereignty because that belongs exclusively to God. The ultimate struggle behind these chaotic seven years of tribulation is the conflict between Satan and his followers and the God of Heaven and His Son, Jesus Christ.

To begin our study on the series of judgments, we must go back to Revelation chapter 5. Very prominent in the early verses of this chapter is a book or scroll that John sees in the hand of the One sitting on the throne.

> And I saw in the right hand of him that sat on the throne a book written within and on the backside, sealed with seven seals. (Rev. 5:1)

This book is vital in relation to all that is about to happen concerning the series of judgments. This book is actually *The Title Deed to All the Earth*. We might think of it as being a "will" or "document of inheritance." The situation is, the earth is filled with wickedness; God's creation has become terribly corrupt; this book contains the rights to claim or authority over this earth.

Note these details about this vital document:

1. It is in the hand of the Father … as Creator, the earth is His
2. It is written on the inside and outside … nothing more could be added … it is complete and final
3. It is sealed with seven seals … reserved for the right time and person to open

The seals mentioned here are likely fixed to the edges of the scroll and must be broken in order for the document to be opened and the rights to inheritance to be enacted. Some historians tell us that Roman law required a will to be sealed seven times for the document to be considered valid.

John hears an angel ask in a loud voice the all-important question: "Who is worthy to open the book, and to loose the seals thereof?" Look at the response:

> And no man in heaven, nor in earth, neither under the earth, was able to open the book, neither to look thereon. And I wept much, because no man was found worthy to open and to read the book, neither to look thereon. (Rev. 5:3-4)

Neither John, nor the angels, nor any of the raptured believers in heaven have the rights to claim the earth and restore it to rightful ownership. What an incredible and tragic dilemma! If no one is worthy, the world would continue under the domination of Satan and his forces, wickedness would continue to escalate, and no Kingdom of God would be established on earth. No wonder John wept much!

However, the scene does not end here. Look at the next few verses:

> And one of the elders saith unto me, Weep not: behold, the Lion of the tribe of Juda, the Root of David, hath prevailed to open the book, and to loose the seven seals thereof. And I beheld, and, lo, in the midst of the throne and of the four beasts, and in the midst of the elders, stood a Lamb as it had been slain, having seven horns and seven eyes, which are the seven Spirits of God sent forth into all the earth. And he came and took the book out

of the right hand of him that sat upon the throne. (Rev. 5:5-7)

Jesus Christ—the Son of God, the Savior of the World—takes the book and all of heaven breaks out in celebration. How indeed could we be appalled at the judgments upon the wicked, coming from the Throne of God when we realize that what is happening is Jesus Christ claiming what is rightfully His and perfectly just?

The scene we have just looked at is actually the beginning of fulfillment of a promise made by God to His Son in both the Old and New Testament:

> Ask of me, and I shall give thee the heathen for thine inheritance, and the uttermost parts of the earth for thy possession. (Ps. 2:8)

> God, who at sundry times and in divers manners spake in time past unto the fathers by the prophets, Hath in these last days spoken unto us by his Son, whom **he hath appointed heir of all things**, by whom also he made the worlds (Heb. 1:1-2, emphasis added)

Chapter 6 begins the successive judgments poured out upon the earth. *Successive* means that the opening of the seventh seal brings about the first of the Trumpet Judgments, and the seventh trumpet sounding brings about the first of the Vial or Bowl Judgments.

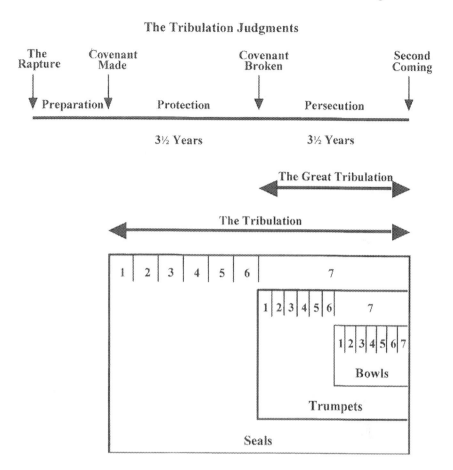

Figure 1. "The Tribulation Judgments" (Constable)

The Seven Seals are Opened – Revelation 6:1-8:1

Views differ concerning the opening of the seven seals as to whether these are separate judgments from the Trumpet and Vial Judgments or if they are instead a broad overview of the other judgments to come. This author leans toward the latter, based on the biblical information being given in more of a general fashion and that the nature of judgments mentioned in this section also parallels the nature of judgments described in the Trumpet and Vial Judgments. Regardless of which view is the most valid, rest assured that everything described in the Seals Judgment will occur at some point of time during the Tribulation.

1. The First Seal – Antichrist Revealed: The White Horse (Rev. 6:2)

   While some hold that this is Christ appearing, stronger evidence introduced earlier suggests that this is, instead, an imitation, the Antichrist. Noteworthy, however, is the Antichrist's appearing at the very beginning of Tribulation events. This is perfectly consistent with the Apostle Paul's instruction to the believers in Thessalonica (2 Thess. 2) that the revealing of "that man of sin," "the son of perdition," "that Wicked" will mark the beginning of the Tribulation Period. His appearance is also the fulfillment of Daniel's prophecy concerning "the prince that shall come."

   > And after threescore and two weeks shall Messiah be cut off, but not for himself: and the people of **the prince that shall come** shall destroy the city and the sanctuary; and the end thereof *shall be* with a flood, and unto the end of the war desolations are determined. (Dan. 9:26, emphasis added)

   Given here is the mission of the Antichrist; that is, he goes forth "conquering and to conquer" (Rev.

6:2). He begins his crusade at the opening of the Tribulation and continues until the whole world is under his domain.

2. The Second Seal – Peace is taken from the earth: Red Horse (Rev. 6:3-4)

    Notice the word "power" in verse four. This word speaks of authority, no doubt a reference to political domination. The political landscape of the Tribulation Period will be that of chaos and total unrest. Jesus mentioned in His sermon that there would be "wars and rumors of wars" (Mat. 24:6).

    > Wherefore I will bring the worst of the heathen, and they shall possess their houses: I will also make the pomp of the strong to cease; and their holy places shall be defiled. Destruction cometh; and they shall seek peace, and *there shall be* none. Mischief shall come upon mischief, and rumour shall be upon rumour; then shall they seek a vision of the prophet; but the law shall perish from the priest, and counsel from the ancients. The king shall mourn, and the prince shall be clothed with desolation, and the hands of the people of the land shall be troubled: I will do unto them after their way, and according to their deserts will I judge them; and they shall know that I *am* the LORD. (Ezek. 7:24-27)

3. The Third Seal – Famine: Black Horse (Rev. 6:5-6)

Americans are very inexperienced when it comes to living with a shortage of food. This scarcity is well known in other parts of the world where the citizens' primary mission every day is merely to find enough food to stay alive. During the Tribulation, this is going to be the case, except on a global scale, and will no doubt result from the warring that will exist, coupled with the judgments that will be targeted toward natural resources.

In John's day, a penny (valued at about 15 cents in today's market) would be a day's wages. A penny (day's wage) would buy one measure of wheat … about enough for one meal. If the person buys barley, a cheaper grain, he could have three meals. However, after one uses his entire day's wage to buy the grain, there would be nothing left to buy the oil or the wine, considered necessities in biblical times. Thus, people will be working to supply only the bare necessities, and those will be in short supply.

4. The Fourth Seal – Death: Pale Horse (Rev. 6:7-8)

Mass killings and death are shocking and tragic to any culture. During the Tribulation, death will be commonplace. Here a fourth of the population will die. By today's population standards, this would be over 1.5 billion people.

The Bible details the methods of death: sword (war), hunger (famine), death (probably disease related), and beasts of the earth (wild animal attacks).

5. The Fifth Seal – Souls of the Martyrs Heard (Rev. 6:9-11)

This scene is in heaven where the souls of those who were martyred during the Tribulation have gone after death. Theirs is an age-old question: "How long, O Lord?" These martyrs are all too aware of just how violent the earth is and just how wicked society has become. The answer they are given is ... not yet. It is not yet time for Jesus Christ to thrust in the sickle and reap the grapes of God's wrath. However, that time is coming!

Notice this tidbit of beauty in the passage. These Tribulation martyrs are given white robes to wear ... robes of righteousness. They have come out of great persecution, distress, hunger, lack of necessities, and have even suffered death because of their holding to the Word of God and their testimony. Now, they are in the presence of God and are robed in His garments of reward.

6. The Sixth Seal – Chaos (Rev. 6:12-17)

John's attention is once again directed to the scene on earth as the sixth seal is opened. The scene here is likely to take place at the very end of the Tribulation, just before Jesus returns with His saints to end it all.

Some of these catastrophic events will be a part of the later Vial Judgments. Notice briefly some shocking happenings that lead to the triumphant appearance of Jesus:

- A great earthquake
- The sun is blackened
- The moon becomes as blood
- The stars from heaven fall
- The heavens are rolled back
- All men, including kings and mighty men, run to the mountains and cry out for them to fall on them and hide them from God

7. The Seventh Seal – Beginning of the Trumpet Judgments (Rev. 8:1)

A very interesting thing happens at the opening of seventh seal. Verse 1 says that there was "silence in heaven about the space of half an hour." No further explanation is given, and we need not speculate as to why this happens. The saints have ceased from their songs of praise; the voice of the martyrs is no longer heard in their cry for action; the sound of angel wings beating the air is no longer heard. It is as if the Great Conductor of the Orchestra has tapped his wand on the music stand of heaven before the instrumentalists, awaiting that first down beat to begin the symphony of the culmination of history as we have known it. Silence in Heaven!

The opening of the seventh seal and the Trumpet Judgments should not be seen as two separate events. The opening of the seventh seal IS the Trumpet Judgments ... the judgments are sequential in nature. The opening of the seventh seal may be well said to mark the beginning of the outpouring of God's wrath and begins the final preparation for the return of Jesus Christ at Armageddon.

The Trumpet Judgments – Revelation 8-11

When the period of silence ends in heaven, John sees seven angels stand before God. To each was given a trumpet, which would be used to sound the announcement and beginning of a specific form of God's wrath being poured out on the earth.

1. The First Trumpet – Hail and Fire (Rev. 8:7)

   This judgment should be taken as being literal hail and fire. Both of these elements have been used by God on occasion in Old Testament passages; for example, the tenth plague that came upon Egypt in Exodus 9:18-26. Interestingly, in the First Trumpet, the fire is mingled with blood. Again, this should be taken as being literal blood.

   The true significance of this judgment is the resulting destruction of one-third of the vegetation on earth, which is burned. This will certainly have an undesirable effect on food supply as well as other industrial involvements that depend on these natural resources.

2. The Second Trumpet – A Mountain of Fire is Cast into the Sea (Rev. 8:8-9)

A blazing mass of some kind falls from heaven and is obviously visible to those within viewing distance. This mass is not a common meteor because it results in a third part of the sea becoming blood—literally. One-third of all marine creatures are killed and one-third of the ships are destroyed. Whether this is speaking of one particular sea or every sea is uncertain. If indeed it affects every sea, then the consequences become even more serious. As with the First Trumpet Judgment, the food supply will be impacted through the losses sustained in the fishing industry.

3. The Third Trumpet – A Star called Wormwood spoils Fresh Water (Rev. 8:10-11)

Somewhat similar to the previous judgment, this is a mass that falls from heaven, yet this one is identified as being a star. The difference is that this star is not blazing and instead of turning the water to blood, it causes the water to be bitter or contaminated. This time the judgment affects the fresh water on the planet. This contaminate must also be poisonous because we are told in verse 11 that men die from drinking the affected water.

With rivers and lakes being scattered across various continents, perhaps this star breaks apart into pieces in the atmosphere and scatters particles across the lands.

Notice that this star is given a name, *Wormwood*. Wormwood is a bitter desert plant mentioned in the Old Testament (Jer. 9:15; 23:15; Amos 5:7) and is always associated with sorrow and bitter judgment.

We see a biblical contrast happening here. In the Old Testament, as the children of Israel were wandering in the wilderness, they came to a place called Marah (Exod. 15). There they found water but the water was bitter. By casting a tree into the bitter waters, the bitter water became sweet. Here Wormwood is cast into the sweet water, and the water becomes bitter.

This judgment will not only affect another source of food for the world's populous, but it also affects its vital water supply. Today, as we live with the threat of terrorists and terrorism, one of the areas of greatest concern is our water-supply systems. If our drinking water supply is compromised, we will have a whole host of resulting problems. Here, one-third of all the earth's fresh water is eliminated from use and could be deadly if consumed.

4. The Fourth Trumpet Judgment – Partial Darkness (Rev. 8:12)

The first three of the Trumpet Judgments has had the desired effect on the land, vegetation, sea, and fresh water. The Fourth Trumpet Judgment affects the heavens. With something like an eclipse effect, the sun, moon, and stars are all partially cut off from their giving of light. Days will likely be shorter and nights longer. We are not told how long this condition continues to exist.

Before moving on to the Fifth Trumpet Judgment, notice that the first four of these Trumpet Judgments have targeted primarily facets of nature: land, vegetation, sea, rivers, and lakes. Nature has been affected not by natural disaster but by supernatural disaster. Though humanity will certainly feel the ramifications of these judgments, humans have not yet been personally targeted. The loss of these things is bad, but at least conditions can remain somewhat tolerable, which changes in verse 13, when John sees and hears an angel flying through the midst of heaven with an urgent and important message. This message is three woes to those who inhabit the earth. A *woe* is a word of lamentable warning, and this series of woes are attached to the next three of the Trumpet Judgments ... the Fifth Trumpet, the Sixth Trumpet, and the Seventh Trumpet containing all seven of the Vial Judgments. Think of it like this: the first four have been bad enough, but the last three will be unimaginable.

5. The Fifth Trumpet Judgment … The First Woe –
   Demonic creatures sent to torture (Rev. 9:1-2)

Our attention is drawn in verse 1 to yet another
"star" that is fallen from heaven. A significant difference
from the one we saw in the Third Trumpet is that this
star is referred to as being a person. The tense of the
verb "fall" indicates that this is a completed action. We
might put it this way: "He has been cast out of heaven."

Most conservative theologians agree that this
person, this star, is none other than Satan himself.
His "fall" here may very well be the occasion that is
recorded for us in Revelation 12:7-9, where he is cast
out of heaven … and seemingly never allowed into the
presence of God again.

> And there was war in heaven: Michael and his
> angels fought against the dragon; and the dragon
> fought and his angels, And prevailed not; neither
> was their place found any more in heaven. And the
> great dragon was cast out, that old serpent, called
> the Devil, and Satan, which deceiveth the whole
> world: he was cast out into the earth, and his angels
> were cast out with him. (Rev. 12:7-9)

Satan unlocks the bottomless pit, or pit of abyss,
and releases "locusts" or demonic beings that have the
power to torture all humans on earth except for the
"sealed servants" of God, probably a reference to the
one hundred forty-four thousand. These locusts have

a sting like that of a scorpion by which they torture people, and for five months they are relentless in their attack. The pain is so severe that human beings will be pleading for death and yet death will not come.

I believe these will be literal demonic beings and their torturous attack will cause literal pain upon all those affected. These demonic beings will have a "king" over them (vs. 11) whose name is Abaddon in the Hebrew and Apollyon in the Greek, which means "destroyer." This king is most likely Satan, as well. Though Americans are somewhat sheltered from demonic activity, make no mistake about it, demons do exist and will be very active during the Tribulation Period.

6. The Sixth Trumpet Judgment ... The Second Woe – Warrior demons sent to kill

In our present age, four demonic beings evidently are bound in the Euphrates River. When the sixth trumpet sounds, these four demonic beings will be released so that they will marshal a huge military of two hundred million soldiers ... likely a literal human army and not demons. These will constitute a massive killing machine that will ultimately destroy a third part of the people on earth.

Some commentators, with merit, have taken the description of the weaponry of this army and made comparisons to modern weapons of our day. John, being obviously unaware of the appearance and abilities of modern weapons (such as tanks and aircraft), may have very well used what he did know—horses, lions, and scorpions—to try to describe the mighty strength and ability of this army.

Such devastation should cause men immediately to turn to God, but it will not. Instead, look at their response to all that is happening:

> And the rest of the men which were not killed by these plagues yet repented not of the works of their hands, that they should not worship devils, and idols of gold, and silver, and brass, and stone, and of wood: which neither can see, nor hear, nor walk: Neither repented they of their murders, nor of their sorceries, nor of their fornication, nor of their thefts. (Rev. 9:20-21)

7. The Seventh Trumpet Judgment … The Third Woe – Beginning of Vial Judgments (Rev. 11:15; 16:1-21)

Chapters 10 through 15 are parenthetical when it comes to chronology of the judgments—with the exception of the announcement of the coming of the third woe and the seventh trumpet in chapter 11, verses 14 and 15.

Quite possibly at this point in the chronology of events, the announcement of the fall of Babylon occurs.

> And there followed another angel, saying, Babylon is fallen, is fallen, that great city, because she made all nations drink of the wine of the wrath of her

fornication. And the third angel followed them, saying with a loud voice, If any man worship the beast and his image, and receive *his* mark in his forehead, or in his hand, The same shall drink of the wine of the wrath of God, which is poured out without mixture into the cup of his indignation; and he shall be tormented with fire and brimstone in the presence of the holy angels, and in the presence of the Lamb: And the smoke of their torment ascendeth up for ever and ever: and they have no rest day nor night, who worship the beast and his image, and whosoever receiveth the mark of his name. (Rev. 14:8-11)

The kingdom of Satan and his Antichrist have fallen apart. The peace that he promised at his coming has long since faded away; the fame that he has acquired has now been turned to distrust and most likely hatred; his political power has now been decimated; his economics have proven to be a failure amidst the conditions that now exist on earth; and his "great empire" is now in the shambles of failure. Revelation 18 gives an expanded description of this devastating fall, which, no doubt, results from the judgments of God that, at this point, have already been executed. God has systematically dismantled the powers of Satan and his desired kingdom. His judgments have not yet ended, however.

At the same time the angel makes the announcement of the fall of Babylon, another angel also appears and pronounces the doom of all those who have followed the beast. Their unholy alliance with this man has proven to be an eternal mistake.

The Vial or Bowl Judgments – Revelation 16

And I saw another sign in heaven, great and marvellous, seven angels having the seven last plagues; for in them is filled up the wrath of God. (Rev. 15:1)

The words *vial* and *bowl* are used interchangeably. The image John is given is that the angels are presented with vessels or bowls containing the "wrath of God." Each will individually pour out the contents of the bowl in successive order.

The Vial Judgments are the last of the judgments and lead to the final battle, Armageddon. All seven of the judgments are covered in Revelation 16, sometimes called *The Great Chapter* because of the repeated use of the word *great* and the severity of the judgments described.

These seven judgments parallel the ten plagues of Egypt, though in greater magnitude, that we find in the book of Genesis. These judgments will likely happen in rapid succession as we come to the end of the Tribulation.

1. The First Vial Judgment – Sores (Rev. 16:2)

   In the plague upon Egypt, these sores were called "boils." The description here is truly painful even to contemplate. The word *noisome* comes from the Greek word meaning "actively causing hurt." The word *grievous* comes from the Greek word meaning "painful, evil, or malignant." Those affected will be the ones who have received the mark of the beast.

   Note that in verses 10 and 11 when the fifth vial is being poured out, these sores are still present … they do not go away.

2. The Second Vial Judgment – Sea becomes blood (Rev. 16:3)

   If you remember the Second Trumpet Judgment, one-third of the sea became blood as a result of the "mountain of fire." Here the entire sea and all the seas become literal blood … a putrefying blood because it is as the blood of a dead man. All sea life is killed.

   One can imagine the catastrophic nature of this event. It will devastate the seafood and industries and make all living conditions along a shoreline of an ocean almost unbearable.

3. The Third Vial Judgment – Fresh Water becomes Blood (Rev. 16:4)

   Just as in the Second and Third Trumpet Judgments where a third part of first the sea and then the fresh water was targeted, now in the Vial Judgments, the same is true. All of the rivers, lakes, and springs are turned into blood, which eliminates all drinking water. Imagine the hostilities that will erupt as the population of the earth starts to suffer from the effects of dehydration and every other ramification of having no available water.

This judgment resembles the first plague upon Egypt (Exod. 7:20-25) where the Nile River is turned into blood, the fish die, and the water is unfit to drink. Here the judgment is global and all sources of water are polluted ... the contaminated water cannot be replenished with fresh water.

We also meet an interesting character in this verse, one called "the angel of the waters." The Revelation records a variety of ministries assigned to the angels. This one evidently has some jurisdiction over the water and points out the justice that this judgment holds in that the wicked have shed the blood of saints (New Testament) and prophets (Old Testament) and therefore they are forced now to drink blood. God will avenge his martyred saints!

This declaration of the angel is joined by another "out of the altar" which offers his Amen to the angel's assessment by saying, *"Even so, Lord God Almighty, true and righteous are thy judgments"* (Rev. 16:7, emphasis added).

4. The Fourth Vial Judgment – The Sun Scorches Men (Rev. 16:8-9)

Like the Fourth Trumpet, this judgment has to do with the effects of the sun. Here the intensity of the sun's heat is increased, causing men to be scorched by its rays. A burn…even sunburn…is perhaps the most painful injury that a person can endure. To make this judgment even harder to tolerate, no source of water is available to these suffering individuals. This torment causes men to blaspheme the name of God.

5. The Fifth Vial Judgment – Darkness on the Antichrist's Kingdom (Rev. 16:10-11)

The "seat of the beast" here is a reference to Jerusalem. The Antichrist has set his throne in the Temple and is ruling as god. The entire region surrounding Jerusalem will be enveloped in total darkness. This judgment parallels the ninth plague on Egypt (Exod. 10:21-23).

This judgment also fulfills two very distinct Old Testament prophecies:

For, behold, the darkness shall cover the earth, and gross darkness the people: but the LORD shall arise upon thee, and his glory shall be seen upon thee. (Isa. 60:2)

Blow ye the trumpet in Zion, and sound an alarm in my holy mountain: let all the inhabitants of the land tremble: for the day of the LORD cometh, for it is nigh at hand; A day of darkness and of gloominess, a day of clouds and of thick darkness, as the morning spread upon the mountains: a great people and a strong; there hath not been ever the like, neither shall be any more after it, even to the years of many generations.... The sun shall be turned into darkness, and the moon into blood, before the great and the terrible day of the LORD come. (Joel 2:1-2 and 31)

6. The Sixth Vial Judgment – River Euphrates Dries Up (Rev. 16:12)

The River Euphrates is on the eastern side of Israel. Drying this river will create a passage for the nations to the east access into the valley of Megiddo. The "kings of the east" mentioned here are literally the kings of the sun rising. These will be Oriental Rulers, including ones from Japan, China, India; and these will likely be joined by Middle Eastern nations.

This judgment will also fulfill the prophecy of Isaiah:

And the LORD shall utterly destroy the tongue of the Egyptian sea; and with his mighty wind shall he shake his hand over the river, and shall smite it in the seven streams, and make men go over dryshod. (Isa. 11:15)

7. The Seventh Vial Judgment – Severe Earthquake and Hail (Rev. 16:17-21)

Perhaps the most powerful words of the Tribulation Period are found here at this last judgment … "It is done!" This judgment is God's grand finale and the last act before the appearing of Jesus Christ.

Note these three parts of this final judgment:

a. Voices, thunder, and lightning out of heaven leave no doubt that what is happening is from God.

b. An earthquake unequalled by any that has ever happened will cause the earth literally to convulse. This event was mentioned by Jesus in His Olivet Discourse:

> Immediately after the tribulation of those days shall the sun be darkened, and the moon shall not give her light, and the stars shall fall from heaven, and the **powers of the heavens shall be shaken** (Mat. 24:29, emphasis added)

- Every city is shattered
- Every island sinks
- Every mountain is flattened

According to the prophecy of Isaiah:

> And they shall go into the holes of the rocks, and into the caves of the earth, for fear of the LORD, and for the glory of his majesty, **when he ariseth to shake terribly the earth**. (Isa. 2:19, emphasis added)

c. Unbelievable hailstones will fall from heaven

Remember that the earthquake has already destroyed all shelter. Houses lie in ruin, buildings have crumbled and fallen, and literally, no place exists for one to run and hide. And now, the heavens open with hailstones the size of which humans have never known. The text says that each hailstone is about the weight of a talent, somewhere between 125 - 135 pounds.

Make no mistake about it ... God is indeed the JUDGE OF ALL THE EARTH! The last word will belong to Him. Even Satan and all his forces pose no match for our Almighty God.

The stage is now set for the greatest battle of all history, the battle of Armageddon.

CHAPTER 4

The Battle of Armageddon

Because of the entrance of sin into the world in the Garden of Eden, humankind has been ceaselessly given to conflict between one another. As the population of the world grew, nations, which now cover the globe, multiplied. With the ever-present plague of sin among these nations, conflict between them has been a constant part of human history. Rarely in the last five thousand years has a war not been taking place somewhere on earth.

However, as we come to the end of human history as we know it, one war will take place that exceeds all others—The Battle of Armageddon.

By the time we come to this period, Babylon (the one-world system) has fallen; the terrors of the Tribulation Period have caused utter chaos; and the Antichrist, empowered by Satan, is in a lame-duck position as his kingdom has been destroyed and the nations of the earth, with no doubt hatred toward him, are clamoring for existence. The Antichrist is in Jerusalem where he has set himself up in the Temple, ruling as god. The nations are now turning on one another and individually turning their attention toward Jerusalem where the Antichrist is.

The Antichrist and the Gathering

The next few pages lay out the events that lead to the battle, though they may not be in chronological order:

1. The River Euphrates dries

    This event happened, as covered previously, at the pouring out of the sixth bowl, allowing the nations of the east a clear passageway into the valley of Megiddo.

    And the sixth angel poured out his vial upon the great river Euphrates; and the water thereof was dried up, that the way of the kings of the east might be prepared. (Rev. 16:12)

    The River Euphrates is the water boundary between the Oriental nations to the east and the Holy Land. The elimination of this obstacle will allow ground troops to move easily into the eastern border of Israel.

2. Demons will entice the kings of all nations to the valley

    And I saw three unclean spirits like frogs *come* out of the mouth of the dragon, and out of the mouth of the beast, and out of the mouth of the false prophet. For they are the spirits of devils, working miracles, *which* go forth unto the kings of the earth and of the whole world, to gather them to the battle of that great day of God Almighty. (Rev. 16:13-14)

Because of the fall of Babylon and extreme judgments that have come, the nations are in complete disarray. Without a doubt, people everywhere are in a survival mode and ready to try to fight their way out of such adverse conditions.

These enticing demons are sent forth unto the kings of the earth from Satan, the Antichrist, and the False Prophet. Their influence is important for this reason: Satan is well aware of the source of this entire catastrophe … God Almighty. Satan is also well versed in the Bible, including the passages that we are looking at, and knows that in the end, a battle with Jesus Christ is inevitable. However, I am convinced that he still thinks he can win. By some form of deceptive spirit, the Antichrist causes the kings of the earth to move their troops into the land of Israel. Perhaps the deception that he uses will be to cause each nation to think that it will have a strategic advantage over other nations and somehow gain national honor or superiority at this point of global weakness.

Another interesting aspect of this gathering of nations is the particular nations involved. We have covered previously the issue of ten kings that are set up by the Antichrist and all ten give their allegiance to him. It is quite likely that the whole structure of global politics is changed during the Tribulation and the domination of the Antichrist. Perhaps there will be absorption of smaller and less powerful countries into these ten primary countries, led by these kings. This kind of structure seems to be consistent with what we know about the end time Babylonian system.

However, three groups are specifically given to us in scripture that we know to be represented here. First is the "kings of the east" or the Oriental or Asian countries. These have been addressed previously.

The second and even more interesting is the nation of Russia. The biblical name for this nation in Ezekiel 38-39 is *Magog* and the end-time leader of the nation is known as *Gog*. There is virtually no debate among scholars that Ezekiel's reference here is present-day Russia.

> And the word of the LORD came unto me, saying, Son of man, set thy face against Gog, the land of Magog, the chief prince of Meshech and Tubal, and prophesy against him, And say, Thus saith the Lord GOD; Behold, I *am* against thee, O Gog, the chief prince of Meshech and Tubal: And I will turn thee back, and put hooks into thy jaws, and I will bring thee forth, and all thine army, horses and horsemen, all of them clothed with all sorts *of armour, even* a great company *with* bucklers and shields, all of them handling swords (Ezek. 38:1-4)

> Therefore, thou son of man, prophesy against Gog, and say, Thus saith the Lord GOD; Behold, I *am* against thee, O Gog, the chief prince of Meshech and Tubal: And I will turn thee back, and leave but the sixth part of thee, and will cause thee to come up from the north parts, and will bring thee upon the mountains of Israel: And I will smite thy bow out of thy left hand, and will cause thine arrows to fall out of thy right hand. Thou shalt fall upon the mountains of Israel, thou, and all thy bands, and

the people that *is* with thee: I will give thee unto
the ravenous birds of every sort, and *to* the beasts
of the field to be devoured. Thou shalt fall upon
the open field: for I have spoken *it*, saith the Lord
GOD. And I will send a fire on Magog, and among
them that dwell carelessly in the isles: and they shall
know that I *am* the LORD. So will I make my holy
name known in the midst of my people Israel; and
I will not *let them* pollute my holy name any more:
and the heathen shall know that I *am* the LORD,
the Holy One in Israel. Behold, it is come, and it is
done, saith the Lord GOD; this *is* the day whereof
I have spoken. (Ezek. 39:1-8)

Russia's involvement is mentioned because in the late
1980s and early 1990s, the nation of Russia seemed to have
been eliminated from the list of major world powers. Many
will remember the words of President Ronald Reagan when he
said, "Tear down this wall." An absence of Russia as a power
would create an issue from a prophetical standpoint since
it is so notable in prophetic passages concerning end times.
However, presently, Russia has once again risen to recognition
as a world power and seems to be gaining in strength with
each passing week. Another piece of the prophetic puzzle is
now in place.

The prophet Daniel adds the third group represented
by mentioning the nations to the south of Israel, probably
African and Arab countries. In context, he is speaking about
the Antichrist and his location in Jerusalem where he is ruling.

The following passage notes that the Antichrist is in a very uncomfortable position in relation to the nations of the earth.

> And at the time of the end shall the king of the south push at him: and the king of the north shall come against him like a whirlwind, with chariots, and with horsemen, and with many ships; and he shall enter into the countries, and shall overflow and pass over. He shall enter also into the glorious land, and many *countries* shall be overthrown: but these shall escape out of his hand, *even* Edom, and Moab, and the chief of the children of Ammon. He shall stretch forth his hand also upon the countries: and the land of Egypt shall not escape. But he shall have power over the treasures of gold and of silver, and over all the precious things of Egypt: and the Libyans and the Ethiopians *shall be* at his steps. But tidings out of the east and out of the north shall trouble him: therefore he shall go forth with great fury to destroy, and utterly to make away many. And he shall plant the tabernacles of his palace between the seas in the glorious holy mountain; yet he shall come to his end, and none shall help him. (Dan. 11:40-45)

3. Jerusalem is attacked

The Seventh Vial Judgment and the earthquake that comes with it split the city of Jerusalem into three parts. The Antichrist is present here as well as many Jewish believers. The forces of the nations have now moved into the region and surround the city of Jerusalem, and the Antichrist seems a major target of their attack. This was prophesied by the prophet Zechariah as well as Christ Himself.

> Behold, I will make Jerusalem a cup of trembling unto all the people round about, when they shall be in the siege both against Judah *and* against Jerusalem. And in that day will I make Jerusalem a burdensome stone for all people: all that burden themselves with it shall be cut in pieces, though all the people of the earth be gathered together against it. (Zech. 12:2-3)

> Behold, the day of the LORD cometh, and thy spoil shall be divided in the midst of thee. For I will gather all nations against Jerusalem to battle; and the city shall be taken, and the houses rifled, and the women ravished; and half of the city shall go forth into captivity, and the residue of the people shall not be cut off from the city. (Zech. 14:1-2)

> And when ye shall see Jerusalem compassed with armies, then know that the desolation thereof is nigh. (Luke 21:20)

4. Jesus appears on the Mount of Olives

Zechariah prophesied this event almost five hundred years before the first coming of Christ. Now it is fulfilled.

Then shall the LORD go forth, and fight against those nations, as when he fought in the day of battle. And his feet shall stand in that day upon the mount of Olives, which *is* before Jerusalem on the east, and the mount of Olives shall cleave in the midst thereof toward the east and toward the west, *and there shall be* a very great valley; and half of the mountain shall remove toward the north, and half of it toward the south. (Zech. 14:3-4)

One possible explanation for Jesus' splitting the Mount of Olives is that the remnant of Jewish believers in Jerusalem may escape out of the city through the resulting passage made. Some scholars also believe that following this appearance, Jesus then goes to two chief cities in Edom, Petra and Bozrah, to gather a hiding remnant of Jews there ... this according to Isaiah 34:6 and 63:1.

5. The armies assemble in the valley of Armageddon

The valley of Armageddon lies to the north of Jerusalem. Perhaps when the troops see Jesus splitting the Mount of Olives, they retreat to the north into this valley, as this is where they end up.

And he gathered them together into a place called in the Hebrew tongue Armageddon. (Rev. 16:16)

The name *Armageddon* comes from two Hebrew words, "har Megiddo" or "hill of Meggiddo." The name *Megiddo* means, "place of troops" or "place of slaughter." It is also called the "Plain of Esdraelon" and "Valley of Jezreel." The valley specifically is 14 miles wide and 20 miles long. The valley itself is the central meeting point, and the armies are scattered for some 200 miles across the region.

This place has been the site of other battles in the past, both in biblical times as well as more recent history:

- Barak defeated the armies of Canaan – Judges 5:19
- Gideon met the Midianites – Judges 7
- King Saul and Josiah were killed here – 1 Samuel 31
- Titus and the Roman armies fought here
- The Crusaders fought here in the Middle Ages
- British General Allenby defeated the Turks – 1917

These massive armies, having had their own ideas of what they had initially thought they were coming to do, must have been shocked and wondering about what these latest developments were all about and what was about to happen.

The True Christ and the Battle

For seven long years, the world has been subject to the ungodly influence and ultimately the domination of the Antichrist and the False Prophet. As the tribulation closes, we will find Jesus

Christ coming to clean up the mess that has been made under this satanic government. In Revelation 5, Jesus is handed the title deed to the earth, as was promised to Him by the Father, and now He is coming to claim that which is rightfully His.

Scripture discloses several elements that will be a part of this divine triumph. The following list may not necessarily be in chronological order; however, they are biblically recorded events in relation to the battle:

1. Darkness covers the earth with quaking

   In the fourth of the Vial Judgments, the sun's strength increases to the point that it scorches people on earth. Now, with the armies gathered in the valley of Armageddon, an opposite effect happens.

   Immediately after the tribulation of those days shall the sun be darkened, and the moon shall not give her light, and the stars shall fall from heaven, and the powers of the heavens shall be shaken (Mat. 24:29)

   One can imagine the consternation that this phenomenon must cause among the troops gathered here. The ground is shaking, there is total darkness, and stars are vanishing. This would cause even the bravest soldier in the world to shiver with fear.

2. The command of judgment is given

   In heaven, all have been waiting for this moment. Back at the opening of the Fifth Seal, we heard the martyred saints of the Tribulation asking the question, "How long O Lord?" Now, it is here!

> And I looked, and behold a white cloud, and upon the cloud *one* sat like unto the Son of man, having on his head a golden crown, and in his hand a sharp sickle. And another angel came out of the temple, crying with a loud voice to him that sat on the cloud, Thrust in thy sickle, and reap: for the time is come for thee to reap; for the harvest of the earth is ripe. And he that sat on the cloud thrust in his sickle on the earth; and the earth was reaped. And another angel came out of the temple which is in heaven, he also having a sharp sickle. And another angel came out from the altar, which had power over fire; and cried with a loud cry to him that had the sharp sickle, saying, Thrust in thy sharp sickle, and gather the clusters of the vine of the earth; for her grapes are fully ripe. And the angel thrust in his sickle into the earth, and gathered the vine of the earth, and cast *it* into the great winepress of the wrath of God. (Rev. 14:14-19)

3. Jesus Christ appears with His saints

Unlike at the rapture, where the redeemed were the only ones who recognized the appearing of Christ, now all will see Him returning.

> And then shall appear the sign of the Son of man in heaven: and then shall all the tribes of the earth

mourn, and they shall see the Son of man coming in the clouds of heaven with power and great glory. (Mat. 24:30)

Behold, he cometh with clouds; and every eye shall see him, and they *also* which pierced him: and all kindreds of the earth shall wail because of him. Even so, Amen. (Rev. 1:7)

Perhaps the most powerful chapter of the Bible is Revelation 19. As a result of the fall of Babylon, a celebration is held to the just and righteous nature of our Lord God. This is followed by the Marriage Supper of the Lamb where the *Redeemed by the Blood* are welcomed around the table of the Lord to celebrate the wedding of Christ and His church. Then, we are given the most descriptive account recorded of the Second Coming of Jesus Christ:

And I saw heaven opened, and behold a white horse; and he that sat upon him *was* called Faithful and True, and in righteousness he doth judge and make war. His eyes *were* as a flame of fire, and on his head *were* many crowns; and he had a name written, that no man knew, but he himself. And he *was* clothed with a vesture dipped in blood: and his name is called The Word of God. And the armies *which were* in heaven followed him upon white horses, clothed in fine linen, white and clean. And out of his mouth goeth a sharp sword, that with it he should smite the nations: and he shall rule them with a rod of iron: and he treadeth the winepress of the fierceness and wrath of Almighty God. And he hath on *his* vesture and on his thigh a name written, KING OF KINGS, AND LORD OF LORDS. (Rev. 19:11-16)

Earlier we noted that a total darkness has covered the valley. The soldiers are overcome by fear and struggling about in this blackness. All of a sudden, heaven opens and out comes Jesus Christ on a white horse, glowing in the splendor of the glory of God. His massive army of millions upon millions of saints from all the ages follows, all riding white horses and wearing royal robes of white. Little more needs to be said about the dramatic effect such a sight will create.

What the Conqueror and the Conquest are going to look like is worth exploring.

The Names Given to Christ

First, He is called "Faithful and True" (Rev. 19:11), as compared to the Antichrist who is unfaithful and false. We are told that he also has an unknown name, possibly the one mentioned in Revelation 3:12.

Him that overcometh will I make a pillar in the temple of my God, and he shall go no more out: and I will write upon him the name of my God, and the name of the city of my God, *which is* new

Jerusalem, which cometh down out of heaven from my God: and *I will write upon him* my new name. (Rev. 3:12)

He is called "The Word of God" in verse 13. John is the only New Testament writer to refer to Jesus as being "The Word." He did so in The Gospel of John and also in The Revelation. Notice that Jesus is not just *a word*, but He is "The Word." A word is made up of letters; and Jesus Christ is the "alpha and omega." He is the Divine Alphabet of God's revelation to us.

In John 1:1-3, John writes, *"In the beginning was the Word, and the Word was with God, and the Word was God. The same was in the beginning with God. All things were made by him; and without him was not anything made that was made"* (emphasis added). In John 1, Jesus Christ is the agent of creation; in Revelation 19 He is the agent of consummation.

Finally, Jesus is called "KING OF KINGS AND LORD OF LORDS" (Rev 19:16). This is His Victorious Name! He is not just a king, but He is the King of all kings. He is not just a lord, but He is the Lord of all lords. This title speaks of Christ's sovereignty, for all kings and lords must submit to Him.

The Description of Christ

His head and *his* hairs *were* white like wool, as white as snow; and his eyes *were* as a flame of fire (Rev. 1:14)

His hair speaks of Him as being the "Ancient of days" (Dan. 7:22), the Eternal One. His eyes speak of searching judgment, the One who sees all and whose attention nothing can escape.

On His head are "many crowns" ... *diadems* (Rev. 19:12). These indicate His magnificent rule and sovereignty. Remember, the false Christ from the First Seal had a crown, but it was not a *diadem*.

His vesture or His garment is "dipped in blood" (Rev. 19:13). This is not His blood but the symbol of the victories that He has already won ... the blood of His foes.

Christ's Mighty Armies

When Christ returns, He will not return alone. Though He will neither need nor use the help of those who return with Him, they are there because of their identification with Him.

A. He returns with His angels (vs. 17)

> When the Son of man shall come in his glory, and all the holy angels with him, then shall he sit upon the throne of his glory (Mat. 25:31)

> And to you who are troubled rest with us, when the Lord Jesus shall be revealed from heaven with his mighty angels, In flaming fire taking vengeance on them that know not God, and that obey not the gospel of our Lord Jesus Christ (2 Thess. 1:7-8)

B. He returns with His saints (vs. 14)

> To the end he may stablish your hearts unblameable in holiness before God, even our Father, at the coming of our Lord Jesus Christ with all his saints. (1 Thess. 3:13)

> When he shall come to be glorified in his saints, and to be admired in all them that believe (because our testimony among you was believed) in that day. (2 Thess. 1:10)

> And Enoch also, the seventh from Adam, prophesied of these, saying, Behold, the Lord cometh with ten thousands of his saints, To execute judgment upon all, and to convince all that are ungodly among them of all their ungodly deeds which they have ungodly committed, and of all their hard *speeches* which ungodly sinners have spoken against him. (Jude 14-15)

These will be the believers from heaven, riding upon matching white horses. This group has already been mentioned in relation to their return with Christ when He comes to judge:

> These shall make war with the Lamb, and the Lamb shall overcome them: for he is Lord of lords, and King of kings: and they that are with him *are* called, and chosen, and faithful. (Rev. 17:14)

Christ's Weapons

The sword that proceeds from His mouth is the Word of God. This is in keeping with the fact that He will consume the enemy with "the spirit of his mouth."

> And then shall that Wicked be revealed, whom the Lord shall consume with the spirit of his mouth, and shall destroy with the brightness of his coming (2 Thess. 2:8)

> But with righteousness shall he judge the poor, and reprove with equity for the meek of the earth: and he shall smite the earth with the rod of his mouth, and with the breath of his lips shall he slay the wicked. (Isa. 11:4)

The "rod of iron" speaks of His strong form of justice as He rules over the earth.

> And he shall rule them with a rod of iron; as the vessels of a potter shall they be broken to shivers: even as I received of my Father. (Rev. 2:27)

> And she brought forth a man child, who was to rule all nations with a rod of iron: and her child was caught up unto God, and *to* his throne. (Rev. 12:5)

Scripture mentions no weapons in the hands of the angels or the saints ... Judgment is reserved for Jesus Christ alone!

1. The bloodiest battle in human history occurs

> And I saw an angel standing in the sun; and he cried with a loud voice, saying to all the fowls that fly in the midst of heaven, Come and gather yourselves together unto the supper of the great God; That ye may eat the flesh of kings, and the flesh of captains, and the flesh of mighty men, and the flesh of horses, and of them that sit on them, and the flesh of all *men, both* free and bond, both small and great. And I saw the beast, and the kings of the earth, and their armies, gathered together to make war against him that sat on the horse, and against his army. (Rev. 19:17-19)

> And the winepress was trodden without the city, and blood came out of the winepress, even unto the horse bridles, by the space of a thousand *and* six hundred furlongs. (Rev. 14:20)

1600 furlongs is about 200 miles. As noted earlier, the Valley of Armageddon is some 20 miles long, indicating that the carnage extends beyond the valley, likely to the north as well as to the south of the valley particular. This will indeed be an enormous battlefield.

Much debate has occurred concerning the bloodshed mentioned in this last verse. Some hold that the blood spilled will literally be pooled and that the depth of it will be four to five feet deep for all 200 miles mentioned. Others hold the same view, except that this depth will only be found in places along this stretch of geography. Still others hold that "unto the horse bridles" speaks of a "splattering" of the blood (similar to the squirting of grapes being trampled in a winepress) to this height and is spread for the length of 200 miles. The language of the verse does not make clear which of these theories is the most valid. The lack of clarity we find here may be the creation of one those mysteries never solved until we see it first-hand.

Look back one more time to the prophet Zechariah for another bit of information concerning the sights on this battlefield.

> And this shall be the plague wherewith the LORD will smite all the people that have fought against Jerusalem; Their flesh shall consume away while they stand upon their feet, and their eyes shall consume away in their holes, and their tongue shall consume away in their mouth. (Zech. 14:12)

The description here sounds much like the same effects of a nuclear explosion. Because of this, some have speculated that there will be some form of nuclear weapon involvement at some point of the battle. Where, if any place, this would fit would be hard-pressed to validate. Granted, God could cause the same thing to happen without the use of a manufactured weapon.

2. Jesus is VICTORIOUS!

> And the beast was taken, and with him the false prophet that wrought miracles before him, with

which he deceived them that had received the mark of the beast, and them that worshipped his image. These both were cast alive into a lake of fire burning with brimstone. And the remnant were slain with the sword of him that sat upon the horse, which *sword* proceeded out of his mouth: and all the fowls were filled with their flesh. (Rev. 19:20-21)

The end of the battle means that Jesus Christ is now returned to establish His Kingdom on earth. We will explore next what we know biblically about that Kingdom as well as how it ends and what our eternal home will be like.

CHAPTER 5

The Eternal State

Our ability to comprehend reality is limited by our finite human minds. We can only truly take in what our five senses inform us of. However, beyond our present and comprehensible environment lies another that is far more elaborate than anything we have thus far realized ... ETERNITY.

Having completed our study of the rapture through the Battle of Armageddon, we now come to what the Bible has to say about our eternal future. In this study, we are going to deal briefly with three future realities: The Millennium, The Lake of Fire, and The New Jerusalem.

Imagine that you were living during the time of Isaiah the prophet. You hear him speak about the coming of the Messiah to be the Savior of the world; you read the words of King David that predict his predecessor who will come to be crucified (Ps. 22) yet live again as the Shepherd of His sheep (Ps. 23) and ultimately be recognized as the "King of Glory" (Ps. 24). These among other prophecies concerning the first coming of Christ may indeed seem to you as being far-fetched and mystical from your vantage point in history. In your mind, there may well be some lingering doubt about these things ever being a reality.

However, from our present time of existence, we can look back and point to the specific times and places where all prophecies concerning the birth, life, death, resurrection, and ascension of Jesus Christ took place as recorded in our New Testament. We can say with assurance that the Old Testament prophets and prophecies were accurate, God-given, and completed just as they had said.

Today, we live in an era where much biblical information is known and documented as being fact according to history. We can read from Genesis 1 through Revelation 3 and say, "Amen!" … "I have no doubt!" Beginning in Revelation 4 and forward, we read of things that are yet to happen: the rapture, the tribulation, Armageddon, and the eternal future. We stand much like Isaiah's contemporaries hearing of things that are yet to be. I am confident that just as the prophecies concerning the first coming of Jesus truly and literally happened, the things that we are about to see will one day truly and literally happen as well.

The Millennial Kingdom

The word *millennium* is a Latin term that simply means "one thousand years." The primary mention of this period is found in Revelation 20 where the first seven verses reference this "thousand years" at least six times: " …*and they* [saints of God] *lived and reigned with Christ a thousand years*" (Rev. 20:4, emphasis added). Three prominent theological positions exist concerning the Millennial Kingdom:

1. Postmillennialism

   The postmillennialist holds the position that through preaching the gospel, the world will eventually embrace Christianity and become a society of saints. When the world has been evangelized, Christ will return and begin to reign over a purified planet. He holds that the thousand years will be literal but will not happen until the world becomes a pure and peaceful place.

The problem with this position is both biblical and historical. The Bible teaches that the coming of Christ will happen after the world has become worse and worse, not better and better (1 Tim. 4:1; 2 Tim. 3:1-5). Historically, we do not see the world getting better; instead, we see a definite downward spiral of world conditions when it comes to peace, morality, and every other attribute consistent with what reigning with Christ would look like.

2. Amillennialism

The amillennialist will say that there will be no thousand-year reign at all (the prefix *a* means "no," hence "no millennium"). He will teach that the church receives all the spiritual promises and prophecies of the Old Testament given to Israel. Amillennialism holds that the word *thousand* is only symbolic, meaning a long period of time and that the glorious description of the Millennial Period in Isaiah and other passages should be explained as being spiritual, not literal. This in essence would mean that we are living today in the Millennial Kingdom.

This position allegorizes scripture and its intended meaning, which is gravely dangerous. There is no reason that we should not take Revelation 20:4 (the declaration of a thousand year reign with Christ) or the beautiful Isaiah 11 description of that reign as being anything but literal.

3. Premillennialism

This view is the oldest (held during the apostolic period and by early church fathers) and most scripturally supported position of the three. The premillennialist holds that Jesus returns at the end of the Tribulation Period to wage a victorious war over wickedness (Battle of Armageddon) and then sets up His earthly and literal Kingdom, which lasts for one thousand years where He Himself will reign as King. I confidently hold to a premillennial position.

For centuries, people have dreamed of and sought for a utopia on earth. Because the efforts revolved around one person's or a group of persons' concept of such a place, those plans were incredibly flawed. In most cases this resulted in a forced submission of the people to the rules and regulations of that existence, ultimately creating more rebellion, violence, and turmoil than had existed before the venture began. Human history teaches us that sinful humanity is incapable of creating and sustaining a paradise on earth. Jesus, however, is not a sinful man or bound by human misconception or frailty.

By the time we come to the Millennial Reign, wickedness has been judged and Satan has been bound in the "bottomless pit" (Rev. 20:2-3). Satan has been the supreme tempter, beginning in the Garden of Eden and continuing through the countless ages. Even during Jesus' earthly ministry, he was at large and busily creating havoc on earth—especially around the ministry of Jesus. The thought of Satan no longer being a contender is enough to make this new kingdom a very desirable place. Here are a few biblical precepts concerning the Millennial Kingdom:

1. The Millennial Kingdom is plainly spoken of in scripture

   One mention in scripture of this kingdom would be enough to substantiate that it will exist. However, its repeated mention affirms that God wants us to know the reality of it and suggests that we should pay special attention to it.

   And I saw thrones, and they sat upon them, and judgment was given unto them: and *I saw* the souls of them that were beheaded for the witness of Jesus, and for the word of God, and which had not worshipped the beast, neither his image, neither had received *his* mark upon their foreheads, or in their hands; and they lived and reigned with Christ a thousand years. But the rest of the dead lived not again until the thousand years were finished.

This *is* the first resurrection. Blessed and holy *is* he that hath part in the first resurrection: on such the second death hath no power, but they shall be priests of God and of Christ, and shall reign with him a thousand years. (Rev. 20:4-6)

The "thousand years" is referenced three times in these three verses. The preceding two verses and the verse that immediately follows mentions the "thousand years" three more times, as it relates to Satan being bound. No reason or principle in scripture interpretation suggests we take this phrase as anything other than a literal one thousand years. When we add the many other scriptural references to the description of a coming kingdom, then it makes perfect sense that the kingdom will exist literally and with all the glory it is described to possess.

2. Jesus taught us to pray for the Millennial Kingdom

During His earthly ministry, the disciples of Jesus asked Him to teach them to pray as John had taught his disciples. Both Matthew and Luke record in similar words Jesus' response.

After this manner therefore pray ye: Our Father which art in heaven, Hallowed be thy name. Thy kingdom come. Thy will be done in earth, as *it is* in heaven. (Mat. 6:9-10)

This prayer has often been referred to as The Lord's Prayer and has been memorized and recited by a vast majority of Christians. Interestingly, Jesus was teaching His disciples to pray, and immediately following the salutation to God as our "Father," the first request of this model prayer was *"thy kingdom come"* and *"thy will be done in earth, as it is in heaven"* (emphasis added). When the Millennial Kingdom begins, this prayer will have been answered. The "kingdom" that Jesus references must be the Millennial Kingdom because it will not be until then that the will of God will fill the earth.

Jesus taught us that we should be praying for the kingdom to come. This prayer should be at the top of our prayer list, for when we pray this way, we can rest assured that it will be answered ... His Kingdom will come!

3. The Millennial Kingdom will fulfill the Abrahamic Covenant

God is not finished with the people of Israel. Though for more than 2,000 years now they have been scattered and living in a dimmed spiritual understanding, a day will come when they will be fully front-and-center of global attention. In Genesis 12, God made a promise to Abraham and his "seed." His promise involved two things: a people forever and a land forever. The Millennial Kingdom will be the ultimate fulfillment of God's promise.

The geographical center of the Millennial Kingdom will be the land of Israel, every place that the sole of Abraham's feet touched, and the capital will be Jerusalem. For the first time, Israel will fully possess all the land promised to Abraham in Genesis 15:18-21. The tribes of Israel will be divided and given possession of the land (Ezek. 37:26-28; 48:1-35). This will indeed be a glorious day for Israel.

> And it shall come to pass in the last days, *that* the mountain of the LORD'S house shall be established in the top of the mountains, and shall be exalted above the hills; and all nations shall flow unto it. And many people shall go and say, Come ye, and let us go up to the mountain of the LORD, to the house of the God of Jacob; and he will teach us of his ways, and we will walk in his paths: for out of Zion shall go forth the law, and the word of the LORD from Jerusalem. And he shall judge among the nations, and shall rebuke many people: and they shall beat their swords into plowshares, and their spears into pruninghooks: nation shall not lift up sword against nation, neither shall they learn war any more. O house of Jacob, come ye, and let us walk in the light of the LORD. (Isa. 2:2-5)

> But in the last days it shall come to pass, *that* the mountain of the house of the LORD shall be established in the top of the mountains, and it shall be exalted above the hills; and people shall flow unto

it. And many nations shall come, and say, Come, and let us go up to the mountain of the LORD, and to the house of the God of Jacob; and he will teach us of his ways, and we will walk in his paths: for the law shall go forth of Zion, and the word of the LORD from Jerusalem. And he shall judge among many people, and rebuke strong nations afar off; and they shall beat their swords into plowshares, and their spears into pruninghooks: nation shall not lift up a sword against nation, neither shall they learn war any more. But they shall sit every man under his vine and under his fig tree; and none shall make *them* afraid: for the mouth of the LORD of hosts hath spoken *it*. (Mic. 4:1-4)

For ages, Israel has been maligned and mistreated. Jerusalem has been the sore spot for many nations. God has not forgotten what He has promised to His people and will one day fulfill His promise in grand fashion. According to Ezekiel 48:35, Jerusalem will be the crown jewel of the kingdom and will be called, *Jehovah-Shammah* meaning, "the Lord is there."

4. The Millennial Kingdom will fulfill the Davidic Covenant

David, the Old Testament patriarch, is certainly one of the most prominent of all biblical characters. From a humble start (1 Sam. 16), God selected him, used him, protected him, and raised him to become the most notable of all of Israel's kings. However, the greatest of David's claims to fame has happened not during his lifetime but instead concerning the One who was promised to come forth as a royal successor to his throne … Jesus Christ.

God's promise to David was that He, God, will establish the throne of David as an everlasting kingdom (2 Sam. 7:12-16; 2 Chron. 13:5) through the "seed" of David, meaning his offspring. One of the reasons the genealogy of Matthew's gospel is so important is because he traces the line of Jesus, through Mary, back to David and ultimately to Abraham.

The book of the generation of Jesus Christ, the son of David, the son of Abraham. (Mat. 1:1)

When the angel appeared to Mary to announce that she was God's chosen vessel to give birth to Jesus the Messiah, a crucial statement within that announcement was that Jesus would be given the *"throne of his father David"* (Luke 1:32, emphasis added).

And, behold, thou shalt conceive in thy womb, and bring forth a son, and shalt call his name JESUS. He shall be great, and shall be called the Son of the Highest: and the Lord God shall give unto him the throne of his father David: And he shall reign over the house of Jacob for ever; and of his kingdom there shall be no end. (Luke 1:31-33)

Jesus made it clear in His teachings while on earth that His kingdom was yet to come. The Jewish people, including the disciples of Jesus, were looking and hoping for Him to set up the kingdom and begin His reign immediately. The plan of God, however, included many prophecies that must be fulfilled (many of which we have previously discussed) before the establishment of the kingdom could occur. The Millennial Kingdom will be the fulfillment of this promise to David, Mary, and all the household of Israel.

5. Individuals in mortal bodies will live during the Millennial Kingdom

Those who have been saved during the Tribulation Period and survive the Battle of Armageddon will enter the Millennial Kingdom in fleshly, mortal bodies (see Isa. 11:10-12). These will bear children during the thousand years, and the population among this group will likely soar. Children born during this time will still have a sin nature and must be saved by believing on Jesus just as we do today. The difference will be that Jesus will be living on earth at this time. The fact that Satan leads a revolt at the end of the Millennial Kingdom and the number of people he involves "*is as the sand of the sea*" (Rev. 20:7-8, emphasis added) evidences this.

6. The Millennial Kingdom will bring tranquility and peace on earth

Though much about living conditions during this period remains unknown, the Bible hints of certain elements of life during the Millennium. Absolute peace will exist among the nations. Jesus Christ will reign over the earth, and all people will be subservient to His rule and unified under His authority. Sin will be quickly and righteously judged by Jesus.

> And there shall come forth a rod out of the stem of Jesse, and a Branch shall grow out of his roots: And the spirit of the LORD shall rest upon him, the spirit of wisdom and understanding, the spirit of counsel and might, the spirit of knowledge and of the fear of the LORD; And shall make him of quick understanding in the fear of the LORD: and he shall not judge after the sight of his eyes, neither reprove after the hearing of his ears: But with righteousness shall he judge the poor, and reprove with equity for the meek of the earth: and he shall smite the earth with the rod of his mouth, and with the breath of his lips shall he slay the wicked. And righteousness shall be the girdle of his loins, and faithfulness the girdle of his reins. (Isa. 11:1-5)

> And he shall judge among the nations, and shall rebuke many people: and they shall beat their

swords into plowshares, and their spears into pruninghooks: nation shall not lift up sword against nation, neither shall they learn war any more. (Isa. 2:4)

Even nature will be altered from its current ability to inflict harm and cause fear among the earth and its inhabitants.

The wolf also shall dwell with the lamb, and the leopard shall lie down with the kid; and the calf and the young lion and the fatling together; and a little child shall lead them. And the cow and the bear shall feed; their young ones shall lie down together: and the lion shall eat straw like the ox. And the sucking child shall play on the hole of the asp, and the weaned child shall put his hand on the cockatrice' den. They shall not hurt nor destroy in all my holy mountain: for the earth shall be full of the knowledge of the LORD, as the waters cover the sea. (Isa. 11:6-9)

Not since the Garden of Eden has the world known the ability to go any place of one's choosing without any fear of danger. Neither has any parent had the luxury of absolute peace of mind that his child will not be harmed by a wild beast or serpent while at play. Freedom from fear will no doubt be one of the greatest benefits of the thousand-year reign of Christ.

7. Jesus Christ will reign as King and we will reign with Him

Life in the present for the child of God is no doubt the greatest life that can be lived. We have the assurance of God's love and care; we have the presence of the indwelling Holy Spirit to comfort and guide; we have the promise of being with Christ when we die. The kingdom of Christ at present is a spiritual kingdom and is *in* us. During the Millennial Reign, however, His kingdom will be physical and will be *with* us.

> The word that Isaiah the son of Amoz saw concerning Judah and Jerusalem. And it shall come to pass in the last days, *that* the mountain of the LORD'S house shall be established in the top of the mountains, and shall be exalted above the hills; and all nations shall flow unto it. And many people shall go and say, Come ye, and let us go up to the mountain of the LORD, to the house of the God of Jacob; and he will teach us of his ways, and we will walk in his paths: for out of Zion shall go forth the law, and the word of the LORD from Jerusalem. (Isa. 2:1-3)

Can you imagine the awesome thrill and privilege of being able to go into the presence of Jesus Christ, to hear His words, to worship in His presence, and to bask in His glory without anything to encumber? He will establish His throne in Jerusalem, and we will have total access to the physical person of Jesus ... we in our glorified bodies that are like His.

Isaiah also gives us a little glimpse of what this will be like:

> And in that day thou shalt say, O LORD, I will praise thee: though thou wast angry with me, thine anger is turned away, and thou comfortedst me. Behold, God *is* my salvation; I will trust, and not be afraid: for the LORD JEHOVAH *is* my strength and *my* song; he also is become my salvation. Therefore with joy shall ye draw water out of the wells of salvation. And in that day shall ye say, Praise the LORD, call upon his name, declare his doings among the people, make mention that his name is exalted. Sing unto the LORD; for he hath done excellent things: this *is* known in all the earth. Cry out and shout, thou inhabitant of Zion: for great *is* the Holy One of Israel in the midst of thee. (Isa. 12:1-6)

Presently, we walk by faith, but then we will walk by sight; now, we look forward with hope, but then we will experience reality; for a little while, we live with sorrow, fear, temptation, and hardships, but then we will live in perfect rest. The good news is that this will last for one thousand years ... and then it gets even better!

Isaac Watts, sometimes known as the "Father of English Hymnody," was the author of over 750 hymns, many of which Christian worship circles still use today. One of his most notable is a song sung almost exclusively around the Christmas season, "Joy to the World," first published in 1719. Interestingly, he wrote this song not as a Christmas hymn, but instead as a response to Psalm 98, which relates to the time when Messiah will rule and reign on earth; we would call this the Millennial Kingdom. This hymn mentions nothing about Christ's incarnation or birth but is filled with attributes of His kingdom on earth. Read again the words of this hymn with the Millennial Kingdom in mind and his actual message becomes very clear.

Joy to the World

Joy to the world, the Lord is come!
Let earth receive her King;
Let every heart prepare Him room,
And heav'n and nature sing,
And heav'n and nature sing,
And heav'n and heav'n and nature sing.

Joy to the earth, the Savior reigns!
Let men their songs employ;
While fields and floods, rocks, hills, and plains
Repeat the sounding joy,
Repeat the sounding joy,
Repeat, repeat, the sounding joy.

No more let sins and sorrows grow,
Nor thorns infest the ground;
He comes to make His blessings flow,
Far as the curse is found,
Far as the curse is found,
Far as, far as the curse is found.

He rules the world with truth and grace,
And makes the nations prove
The glories of His righteousness,
And wonders of His love,
And wonders of His love,
And wonders, wonders of His love.

We need to note here that according to Revelation 20:7-9, at the end of the thousand years, Satan will be loosed for short time. He will compass the earth to recruit individuals who have been born during the Millennium and have not believed on Jesus Christ for salvation for a final revolt against God. These will have mortal bodies with sinful natures who evidently resist the righteous rule of Christ. No evidence suggests that we as present-day believers will be susceptible to his deception or may possibly be led astray by him. Remember, we will then be in glorified bodies.

The number of those Satan assembles is compared to *"the sand of the sea,"* a mighty army indeed (emphasis added). The target of this army is the saints of God, the city of Jerusalem, and Gog and Magog. As we learned in the previous chapter, most believe that Gog and Magog refer to Russia and the Russian leader. However, because of the timing of the event and the means whereby they are destroyed, this cannot be one and the same invasion. It will likely be a revived form of the previous Russian-led attack (described in Ezek. 38-39) which will have happened at the Battle of Armageddon.

The only explanation as to why Satan is released for this period of time is that it proves what the scripture says that the condition of the unregenerate heart of man is "desperately wicked" (Jer. 17:9). Even under the perfect and ideal reign of Jesus Christ, the natural man remains at enmity against God. Here is a final test, will a thousand years with Christ on earth be singularly enough to change a carnal heart? Satan finds a massive group that gives evidence that it is not. Sadly and eternally, those who reject Jesus suffer the consequences for their rejection of God's free gift.

God will send fire from heaven to destroy this army and will once and for all cast Satan into the lake of fire to be banished forever from the face of the earth.

The Lake of Fire

The Word of God tells us of only two places and two possible destinies where human beings will spend eternity. The New City Jerusalem is the place that is presently being prepared for those who truly believe on Jesus Christ and have made Him the Savior of their souls (John 14:1-6). The Lake of Fire is the only other alternative and, as declared by Jesus, is the place prepared for *"the devil and his angels"* (Mat. 25:41, emphasis added).

Mentioning a place of eternal torment is certainly not a popular thing to do. However, one cannot be honest with scripture and truthful with individuals without a clear and stern warning of their place and all that pertains to it. Reportedly, scripture mentions hell more often than heaven, which communicates the gravity of the subject.

Scripture distinguishes between "hell" (the Greek word is *hades*) and the Lake of Fire: it is clear on the fact that when the unsaved person dies, his soul goes immediately to this place called *hades* (Luke 16:19-31). This is a place of torment, and the soul of the departed remains here until the end of the Millennial Kingdom and the final judgment, the Great White Throne Judgment. The Lake of Fire is the final and eternal place of torment for the devil, his angels, his agents, and all unbelievers.

Revelation 19:20 informs us that at the end of the Battle of Armageddon, the beast (Antichrist) and the false prophet are "cast alive into a lake of fire burning with brimstone." After the final revolt of Satan and the second Battle of Gog and Magog, Satan joins them in this final place of judgment.

> And the devil that deceived them was cast into the lake of fire and brimstone, where the beast and the false prophet *are*, and shall be tormented day and night for ever and ever. (Rev. 20:10)

According to this verse, Satan is cast into the Lake of Fire—over one thousand years after the Antichrist and false prophet have been cast in. Scripture clearly states that they *"are"* still in existence in this place of torment. Further, their torment will last "for ever and ever." Some believe that the Lake of Fire is a place of annihilation: individuals are cast there, destroyed, and cease to exist. Conversely, the scriptures teach that it is a place of eternal torment with no escape or final destruction.

> And if thy hand offend thee, cut it off: it is better for thee to enter into life maimed, than having two hands to go into hell, into the fire that never shall be quenched: Where their worm dieth not, and the fire is not quenched. And if thy foot offend thee, cut it off: it is better for thee to enter halt into life, than having two feet to be cast into hell, into the fire that never shall be quenched: Where their worm dieth not, and the fire is not quenched. And if thine eye offend thee, pluck it out: it is better for thee to enter into the kingdom of God with one eye, than having two eyes to be cast into hell fire: Where their worm dieth not, and the fire is not quenched. (Mark 9:43-48)

At this point, Satan and his agents, the Antichrist and false prophet, are in the Lake of Fire. The unbelievers from the Millennial Kingdom have been killed, and their souls are in *hades*. What follows is what we call The Great White Throne Judgment, taken from this text in Revelation 20.

> And I saw a great white throne, and him that sat on it, from whose face the earth and the heaven fled away; and there was found no place for them. And

> I saw the dead, small and great, stand before God; and the books were opened: and another book was opened, which is *the book* of life: and the dead were judged out of those things which were written in the books, according to their works. And the sea gave up the dead which were in it; and death and hell delivered up the dead which were in them: and they were judged every man according to their works. And death and hell were cast into the lake of fire. This is the second death. And whosoever was not found written in the book of life was cast into the lake of fire. (Rev. 20:11-15)

What occurs here is obviously another resurrection, this time of the bodies of all the unsaved. "Dead" here speaks of those who are spiritually dead and, as the text makes plain, their names are not found in the "*book* of life." These seem to be raised bodily—"the sea gave up the dead which were in it" and "death," likely a reference to the grave and "hell" (*hades*) a reference to the place of the souls of men. The unbelieving from all the ages are brought before the throne of God.

The judgment that is happening here needs attention. First, note that the Judge is none other than God Himself … namely Jesus Christ.

> For as the Father raiseth up the dead, and quickeneth *them*; even so the Son quickeneth whom he will. For the Father judgeth no man, but hath committed all judgment unto the Son: That all *men* should honour the Son, even as they honour the Father.

He that honoureth not the Son honoureth not the Father which hath sent him. Verily, verily, I say unto you, He that heareth my word, and believeth on him that sent me, hath everlasting life, and shall not come into condemnation; but is passed from death unto life. (John 5:21-24)

Make no mistake about it, Jesus Christ is God-In-The-Flesh! To believe on Him is the only recourse to escape the "condemnation" and be brought from "death unto life." Those who are appearing at the Great White Throne Judgment are the ones who have not believed. Now, He is their Judge! This will happen just as Paul described about the exalted position of the once crucified and eternally risen Savior.

Let this mind be in you, which was also in Christ Jesus: Who, being in the form of God, thought it not robbery to be equal with God: But made himself of no reputation, and took upon him the form of a servant, and was made in the likeness of men: And being found in fashion as a man, he humbled himself, and became obedient unto death, even the death of the cross. Wherefore God also hath highly exalted him, and given him a name which is above every name: That at the name of Jesus every knee should bow, of *things* in heaven, and *things* in earth, and *things* under the earth; And *that* every tongue should confess that Jesus Christ *is* Lord, to the glory of God the Father. (Phil. 2:5-11)

Because Jesus Christ is the Judge, the judgment will be absolutely righteous and the punishment will be perfectly just.

Secondly, *"the book of life"* is present. This book is also known as *"The Lamb's Book of Life"* (Rev. 21:27, emphasis added) and contains the names of all who have believed on Jesus Christ (Phil. 4:3; Rev. 3:5; 13:8; 17:8; 22:19). All whose names were not found in this book of life are cast into the Lake of Fire. The answer to one and only question—Is your name in the Lamb's book of life?—determines whether the Lake of Fire is a person's place of eternal destiny.

Next, notice that other books are present at this judgment. These are the books of "works." The lost are shown their works from these books, and these declare their guilt of sin. Lest anyone protest the fact that their name should be in the book of life because of their innocence, their deeds will be disclosed before their very eyes.

> A good man out of the good treasure of the heart bringeth forth good things: and an evil man out of the evil treasure bringeth forth evil things. But I say unto you, That every idle word that men shall speak, they shall give account thereof in the day of judgment. For by thy words thou shalt be justified, and by thy words thou shalt be condemned. (Mat. 12:35-37)

Jesus warned us as well that there would be those who claim their right to escape judgment based on their religious service instead of His shed blood. They also will find that religion does not put their name in the book of life.

> Not every one that saith unto me, Lord, Lord, shall enter into the kingdom of heaven; but he that doeth the will of my Father which is in heaven. Many will say to me in that day, Lord, Lord, have we not prophesied in thy name? and in thy name have cast out devils? and in thy name done many wonderful works? And then will I profess unto them, I never knew you: depart from me, ye that work iniquity. (Mat. 7:21-23)

With guilt established, the unsaved of all the ages now come to the justice they deserve. They remained dead spiritually and now face that *"the wages of sin is death"* (Rom. 6:23, emphasis added). This death is eternal separation from God, forever banished to the same torment that Satan, the Antichrist, and the false prophet are now sharing. What is so sad is that all they had to do was receive the free pardon from God that was purchased by the precious blood of His Son, Jesus.

The New City Jerusalem

Upon purchasing a new car, we often make the comment, "There is nothing like that 'new-car' smell." Can you imagine, however, what it would be like to move into a brand new city, a city that has never yet been populated or polluted, is not crowded or cluttered, and has been designed and built by the Divine Architect of the universe, Jesus Christ?

Dating all the way back to the words of assurance that Jesus gave to His disciples before the crucifixion, the believer has looked forward to His promise that, in spite of all the terribly negative things life may hold, a grand and glorious day and place would one day come.

> Let not your heart be troubled: ye believe in God, believe also in me. In my Father's house are many mansions: if *it were* not *so*, I would have told you. I go to prepare a place for you. And if I go and prepare a place for you, I will come again, and receive you unto myself; that where I am, *there* ye may be also. (John 14:1-3)

Following the Great White Throne Judgment and the eternal banishment of unbelievers to the Lake of Fire, John is immediately given a view of the eternal home of true believers.

Revelation 21 opens with John making the first of three usages of the phrase "I saw" in this chapter. The first thing that he saw was a new heaven and a new earth, because the old heaven and earth has "passed away." The scriptures give little information concerning this transition between the old and new heaven and earth. We do know that it was prophesied as late in time as the writings of the Apostle Peter.

> But the day of the Lord will come as a thief in the night; in the which the heavens shall pass away with a great noise, and the elements shall melt with

fervent heat, the earth also and the works that are therein shall be burned up. *Seeing* then *that* all these things shall be dissolved, what manner *of persons* ought ye to be in *all* holy conversation and godliness, Looking for and hasting unto the coming of the day of God, wherein the heavens being on fire shall be dissolved, and the elements shall melt with fervent heat? Nevertheless we, according to his promise, look for new heavens and a new earth, wherein dwelleth righteousness. (2 Pet. 3:10-13)

The timing of this transition seems to take place after the Millennial Reign and the Great White Throne Judgment. There is no doubt that God has the power and ability to annihilate the old creation and instantly create a new one to take its place. This new creation will be the place where the New City Jerusalem will descend and be the eternal home of all the righteous. This work will not be merely a transformation of the old creation but instead a creation of a totally new one.

John specifically points out in verse 1 that in this new earth there is "no more sea." Our present earth contains seas that cover a majority of its mass. The only mention of water supply is the "pure river of the water of life" spoken of in the opening verses of Revelation 22, and yet we will find that this supply will be quite sufficient. Furthermore, in scripture the analogy of the "sea" is often used in relation to turmoil and strife … in the new earth there is "no more sea."

In Revelation 21:2, John seems to put himself under oath to affirm the reality of this glorious city descending from God out of heaven when he states: "I John." Notice the descriptive terms he uses here concerning what he saw:

- It is a "new Jerusalem" … not the old one restored
    ○ Unlike the first Jerusalem, this one has never been attacked and destroyed; this one has never been occupied by the enemy; this one has never had tour buses and tourists crowd its streets.
- It is a "holy city" … no litter, no congestion, no crime, and the only noise will be that of adoration of saints for their Savior
    ○ This will be the abode of God and His people.
- It is a "prepared" city … described as a beautiful bride on her wedding day

Before we look at a few of the glorious attributes of the city, we need to consider what will not be a part of it:

> He that overcometh shall inherit all things; and I will be his God, and he shall be my son. But the fearful, and unbelieving, and the abominable, and murderers, and whoremongers, and sorcerers, and idolaters, and all liars, shall have their part in the lake which burneth with fire and brimstone: which is the second death. (Rev. 21:7-8)

> And there shall in no wise enter into it any thing that defileth, neither *whatsoever* worketh abomination, or *maketh* a lie: but they which are written in the Lamb's book of life. (Rev. 21:27)

This city will be populated by a perfected people who are submitted to the Perfect King, King Jesus. There will be no need for jails, courthouses, hospitals, nursing homes, or cemeteries. Occupations will be obsolete … judges, lawyers, police officers, soldiers, doctors, counselors, builders, educators, and all the rest … and yes, even preachers because we will have the Living Word living among us.

Perhaps a helpful way to see the change of existence that we will experience is to compare what we know from creation in Genesis to what we will move into in the new city in The Revelation:

Genesis	Revelation
Heavens and earth created (1:1)	New heaven and new earth (21:1)
Sun created (1:16)	No need for the sun (21:23)
The night established (1:5)	No night there (22:5)
The seas created (1:10)	No more seas (21:1)
The curse announced (3:14-17)	No more curse (22:3)
Death enters history (3:19)	No more death (21:4)
Man driven from the tree (3:24)	Man restored to Paradise (22:14)
Sorrow and pain begin (3:17)	No more tears or pain (21:4)

This place we will call "Home" for all eternity is described in Revelation 21:

1. The glory of God is the light of the city – Rev. 21:23

   In our present world, light is of the essence for life to be sustained. God has wisely and graciously given us natural light with the sun, moon, and stars, and nature is preserved through their contributions. In the

New City Jerusalem, however, these will no longer be necessary. Here, not the handiwork of God but God Himself will be the light. He in all His glory will fill the new city with rays of celestial light that obliterates all darkness and provides a clear view of the wonderful place He has prepared for His people.

> The sun shall be no more thy light by day; neither for brightness shall the moon give light unto thee: but the LORD shall be unto thee an everlasting light, and thy God thy glory. Thy sun shall no more go down; neither shall thy moon withdraw itself: for the LORD shall be thine everlasting light, and the days of thy mourning shall be ended. (Isa. 60:19-20)

2. A wall surrounds the city – Rev. 21:12-15; 17-21

The wall spoken of here is not for the purpose of defense because verse 27 states that nothing defiling exists in this city. The wall is more likely an addition to the majesty and glory of the city and perhaps serves as a reminder of the previous city of Jerusalem.

Note a few truly impressive traits of this surrounding wall:

- It is massive in size (vs. 17)
  - The measurement here is no doubt relating to the height of the wall. In today's measurements, 144 cubits would be approximately 216 feet. The wall

completely surrounds the city, standing at this incredible height.

- It is made of jasper (vs. 18)
    - The jasper stone is found in a variety of colors, and the wall may be of any one of these colors or a variety of several. Verse 11 indicates that this wall has a transparency aspect to it ... "clear as crystal." This stone is very costly by today's standard but is used lavishly in the new city.
- It has 12 foundations
    - The foundations mentioned here show us the permanence of the walls and the city. Each of the foundations is garnished with a separate precious stone as listed in verses 19 through 21. According to verse 14, each of the foundations is also inscribed with the names of the Twelve Apostles. This no doubt ties the new city to the New Testament period and saints.
- It has 12 gates
    - Each of the gates is made with one single pearl (vs. 21). John also notes that each gate carries the denotation of each of the 12 tribes of Israel (vs. 12) ... this would tie the city to an identification of the Old Testament period and saints.

- ◦ The designation of the gates could be tied to the description in Ezekiel 48:31-34. If so, then the pattern would look like this:
    - On the north side, going east to west, Levi, Judah, and Reuben
    - On the east side, going from north to south, Joseph, Benjamin, and Dan
    - On the west side, going from north to south, Naphtali, Asher, and Gad
    - On the south side, going from east to west, Simeon, Issachar, and Zebulon

When coupled with the foundation identifications of the Apostles, we can conclude that both Old and New Testament believers are a part of the inhabitants of this city.

- An angel is posted at each of the gates and, according to verse 25, the gates are never shut

3. The city is absolutely remarkable

After considering the awesome view of the walls that surround New Jerusalem, we can have incredibly high expectations of the city itself, and any dashed anticipation is eliminated.

The city is constructed of "pure gold, like unto clear glass" (18). Even the streets of the city are made of "pure gold, as it were transparent glass" (25). In our present world, we do not usually select street material for its beauty. In New Jerusalem, however, even the common areas hold a beauty that here and now the most prestigious palaces would hope to possess even a small portion of.

Given the brightness of the glory of God is the light of the city, one can imagine the spectacular nature of this glorious light reflecting off of the walls, foundations, street, and mansions that make up this remarkable place.

4. The size of the city is enormous

Our current earth is home to some incredibly large cities. Oftentimes these cities with their sprawling masses of streets and buildings are home to several million people. However, none of these cities or all of them put together can match the size of this new city that God has prepared.

John is shown that the shape of the city is "foursquare" (Rev. 21:16); accordingly, its length, breadth, and height are all equal. Think of its appearance as that of a huge cube. Each of the dimensions—length, breadth, and height—measures 12,000 furlongs. One furlong is almost 600 feet; thus, the city is approximately 1,500 miles squared. At its ground level, the city will cover the equivalent to the distance from the farthest part of Maine to the farthest part of Florida and from the east coast of the United States to Colorado—this is only the length and breadth. The city is also 1,500 miles high! The dimensions given calculate to more than two million square miles. As described on RemnantReport. com, astrophysicist Hugh Ross says, "If its population exceeds ten billion, the New Jerusalem alone would give each of us about forty billion cubic feet of space (equivalent to a fourteen square mile home with a hundred foot high ceiling" (qtd. in "New Jerusalem").

While not specifically stated, perhaps the city will consist of layers or levels where we will dwell. If this is the case and every layer or level is 1,000 feet in height, there would be around 7,800 layers. To give you an idea of how much square footage that would provide, if these layers were spread out, they would cover more space than 89 earths in land mass.

Jesus promised His people that He was going to *"prepare a place for [them]"* (John 14:2, emphasis added). This place is certainly far beyond anything we can imagine in beauty, splendor, and size. The greatest part of this promise, however, is what He said next ... *"And if I go and prepare a place for you, I will come again and receive you unto myself; that where I am, there you may be also"* (John 14:3, emphasis added). The true "Spotlight" of New Jerusalem will be JESUS!

Epilogue

The study of prophecy is certainly interesting, especially regarding issues of the last days. No one, including myself, has all the answers to all the questions about this subject. We do have enough biblical information, however, to cause us to dig a little deeper in the Word and seek a little farther for clarity and understanding. My hope is this writing will cause you to do just that.

Learning more about what lies ahead from biblical passages is not for gaining prideful intelligence that will cause us to feel superior or be labeled as an eschatological expert. Diligent study of *Things to Come* should cause us to better our spiritual walk with Christ as well as create an eager anticipation for Jesus' return at the rapture.

> Beloved, now are we the sons of God, and it doth not yet appear what we shall be: but we know that, when he shall appear, we shall be like him; for we shall see him as he is. And every man that hath this hope in him purifieth himself, even as he is pure. (1 John 3:2-3)

> But the day of the Lord will come as a thief in the night; in the which the heavens shall pass away with a great noise, and the elements shall melt with fervent heat, the earth also and the works that are therein shall be burned up. *Seeing* then *that* all these things shall be dissolved, what manner

of persons ought ye to be in *all* holy conversation and godliness, Looking for and hasting unto the coming of the day of God, wherein the heavens being on fire shall be dissolved, and the elements shall melt with fervent heat? Nevertheless we, according to his promise, look for new heavens and a new earth, wherein dwelleth righteousness. Wherefore, beloved, seeing that ye look for such things, be diligent that ye may be found of him in peace, without spot, and blameless. (2 Pet. 3:10-14)

Realizing that the Word of God assures us of the Second Coming also motivates the child of God to be a faithful, ready, and verbal witness for Jesus Christ to reach lost souls before it is too late. The old prophet Daniel, to whom we have looked for several of his end-time prophecies, charges us to be diligent in turning the sinner to the Savior:

And at that time shall Michael stand up, the great prince which standeth for the children of thy people: and there shall be a time of trouble, such as never was since there was a nation *even* to that same time: and at that time thy people shall be delivered, every one that shall be found written in the book. And many of them that sleep in the dust of the earth shall awake, some to everlasting life, and some to shame *and* everlasting contempt. And they that be wise shall shine as the brightness of the firmament; and they that turn many to righteousness as the stars for ever and ever. (Dan. 12:1-3)

I would not assume that every reader of this volume has made spiritual preparation for the coming of the Lord. If you are not sure that if Jesus Christ were to return right now you would be taken to be with Him at the rapture, then I would plead with you to trust Him as Savior here and now. To delay accepting Jesus Christ as Savior is an eternally risky thing to do. If He came right now or your eyes should close in death, then you have crossed the line of opportunity to be saved.

God loves you so much that He has sent His only begotten Son to come to earth, suffer death on the cross as the penalty for your sin, and offer you the free gift of eternal life. For you it is freely given because Jesus has already paid the price.

Here Is How You Can Be Saved

1. Acknowledge that you are a sinner
   For all have sinned, and come short of the glory of God (Rom. 3:23)

2. Admit that because you are a sinner you are deserving of God's wrath
   For the wages of sin *is* death; but the gift of God *is* eternal life through Jesus Christ our Lord. (Rom. 6:23)

3. Believe that God loves you and sent His Son to save you
   But God commendeth his love toward us, in that, while we were yet sinners, Christ died for us. (Rom. 5:8)

4. Call upon Jesus to forgive your sin and become your Savior

> That if thou shalt confess with thy mouth the Lord Jesus, and shalt believe in thine heart that God hath raised him from the dead, thou shalt be saved. For with the heart man believeth unto righteousness; and with the mouth confession is made unto salvation. For the scripture saith, Whosoever believeth on him shall not be ashamed. For there is no difference between the Jew and the Greek: for the same Lord over all is rich unto all that call upon him. For whosoever shall call upon the name of the Lord shall be saved. (Rom. 10:9-13)

I would encourage you to pray from your heart to the heart of God something like this: "God, I am a sinner. I cannot save myself, but I believe that you sent your Son to die for me and save me from my sin. With all my heart, I ask you to forgive me of my sin, come into my life, and save me with the salvation that only you can give. In Jesus' name I pray, Amen."

"Even so, Come, Lord Jesus!" (Rev. 22:20)

Bibliography

Action Against Hunger International. 2015. Web. 01 11 2014.

Constable, Thomas L. "Notes on Revelation: 2014 Edition." 2015. *Soniclight.com.* Web. 6 Feb. 2015.

Falwell, Jerry. *Dr. Jerry Falwell Teaches Bible Prophecy.* Lynchburg, Virginia: The Old-Time Gospel Hour, Inc., 1979. Print.

NATO. *NATO.* n.d. Web. 10 Nov. 2014.

"New Jerusalem: Just a Metaphor?" 2015. *Remnant Report. com.* Web. 18 Nov. 2014.

U.S. Geological Survey. *USGS: Science for a Changing World.* 26 Aug. 2014. Web. Nov. 18 2014.